# Altered Paper JEWELRY

QUARRY

# Altered Paper JEWELRY

BEVERLY MASSACHUSETTS

Artful Adornments from Beautiful Papers

JENN MASON

QUARRY BOOKS

First published in the United States of America by
Quarry Books, a member of
Quayside Publishing Group
100 Cummings Center
Suite 406-L
Beverly, Massachusetts 01915-6101
Telephone: (978) 282-9590
Fax: (978) 283-2742
www.quarrybooks.com

**Library of Congress Cataloging-in-Publication Data**
Mason, Jenn.
  Altered paper jewelry : artful adornments from beautiful papers / Jenn Mason.
     p. cm.
  ISBN 978-1-59253-454-8
  1.  Paper work. 2.  Jewelry making.  I. Title.
  TT870.M37325 2008
  745.594'2—dc22
                              2008015680

ISBN-13: 978-1-59253-454-8
ISBN-10: 1-59253-454-6

10 9 8 7 6 5 4 3 2 1

Design: Laura H. Couallier, Laura Herrmann Design
Cover Image: Lexi Boeger
Illustrations: Judy Love, page 13, 15, 17; Michael Gellatly, page 16
Templates: Jenn Mason

Printed in Singapore

Dedicated to Jen VanSant, who taught me
how to truly live creatively.

# Contents

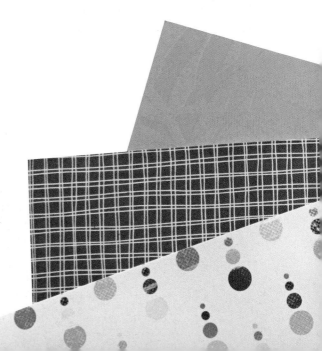

# *Introduction*

## WHAT SHOULD I WEAR TODAY?

For many of us, this is how we start our day. (Which begs the question: if you're not asking yourself this query, do you not care what you're wearing, or are you not wearing clothes?) Depending on our level of consciousness and caffeine intake, this can be a difficult way to begin the morning. But instead of worrying about whether or not the pants you've chosen to wear make your derrière look ample, why not focus on personal embellishments —those little statements you make to people you encounter throughout your day without even saying a word. If the old cliché about second chances and first impressions is true, don't you owe it to yourself to share who you are with the outside world? The accoutrement you choose to adorn yourself with says, "Here I am!" It can also say: I am a person of many layers; I like citrus green; I adore flowers; I have a generous funny bone; or WARNING: I'm in a bad mood today.

If you're new to the world of paper art but enjoy making jewelry, there is no time like right now to start playing with old book pages and gel medium. Use your jewelry-creating skills to push your expectations. Look through the gallery at the end of the book or go to an art museum and be inspired by color and texture. This book will enthusiastically walk you through a number of paper art techniques that you can master in no time.

If you're a paper art junkie, welcome aboard! This book is a journey of techniques and a study in scale—especially since you can't wear the 5" × 7" (12.5 × 18 cm) collages you normally make as earrings. Even if you've never made a necklace in your life, you will be capable of making any of the projects in this book. The added bonus is that you can now wear a piece of your art around your wrist, on your lapel, or gracefully dangling from your ears.

To be even more user friendly, I've rated each project with pliers and scissors. The more pliers indicated, the more involved the jewelry-making aspect of the project; the more scissors you see, the more advanced the paper art technique. Never fear, though; I always keep the beginner in mind—after all, today's beginner is tomorrow's artist. If you are a beginner, just know that the more scissors and pliers you see, the more time a project may take. You *can* do it! (See the key on page 11.)

When you've run out of days to wear all of your fabulous new miniature masterpieces, you can make them for your friends and family. Maybe even Fido, the family mutt, will get a new nametag on his collar.

Read on to see how to make a Mood Swings pendant (page 24), Chandelier Chic earrings (page 66), and a Buckle, Buckle belt (page 70). Or maybe your style leans more to the Domino Effect necklace (page 38) or the Baubled Bangle bracelet (page 46). Each project includes a variation, to help you stretch your imagination. Regardless of your style or favorite type of jewelry, you will be inspired by the gallery at the end of the book. Nineteen artists have contributed beautiful, intriguing works of personal embellishment for your inspiration. Now, grab your scissors, your pliers, and your favorite paper and let's adorn ourselves with art!

"Remember always that you not only have the right to be an individual, you have an obligation to be one."
—*Eleanor Roosevelt*

9

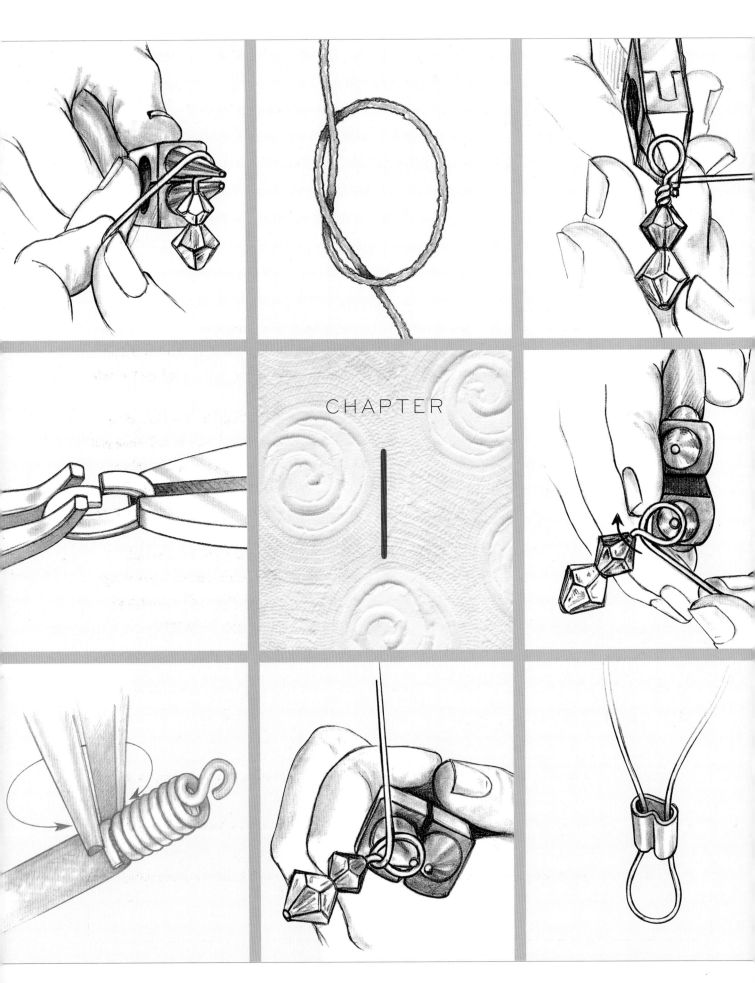

CHAPTER

I

# Tools and Techniques

MAKING ALTERED PAPER JEWELRY REQUIRES ME TO DO A LOT OF flipping back and forth between my jewelry making supplies and my paper art supplies. The transition between the two is fairly easy when you have the right tools—and a place to work.

In this chapter, I'll walk you through the jeweler's studio (as it relates to making altered paper jewelry) and the paper artist's studio. You might already be well equipped in either or both studios, but it never hurts to take inventory of your supplies and see what you might be missing. The supply lists for the Basic Paper Tool Kit and the Basic Jewelry Tool Kit don't include everything—I've whittled them down, to give you a quick start. You can add to them as you see fit.

Following the supply section are a few basic jewelry making techniques with illustrations. If you've never made jewelry before, you'll be amazed at how many things you can make using just these few techniques. Of course, practice makes perfect, so grab a few beads, some head pins, and some wires and start practicing today.

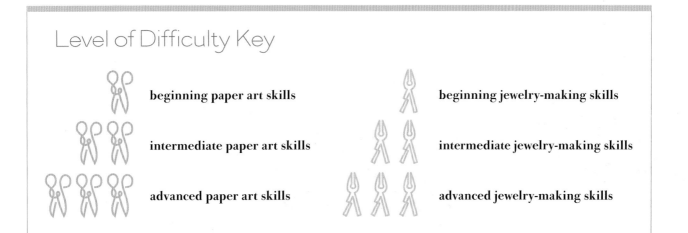

## Level of Difficulty Key

beginning paper art skills    beginning jewelry-making skills

intermediate paper art skills    intermediate jewelry-making skills

advanced paper art skills    advanced jewelry-making skills

# *Inside the Paper Studio*

## Basic Paper Tool Kit

The Basic Paper Tool Kit includes supplies that every paper artist should always have on hand. This kit is listed in the supply section of every project in this book. Some of the other supplies listed below, such as gel mediums, permanent ink, and markers, are also great to include in your Paper Tool Kit.

Following are the recommended supplies for your Basic Paper Tool Kit:

- **scissors** (good-quality large blade and small detail scissors)
- **craft knife** and **cutting mat**
- **glue stick**
- **quick-drying craft glue**
- **paper trimmer**
- **bone folder** – great tool for all sorts of tasks, including folding, scoring, and even clay bead manipulation
- **awl** – a tool with a handle and a sharp, pointed end. It is extremely useful for making beads, poking holes, and other similar tasks.
- **pencil**

Other items to consider:

- **paper** – decorative, double-sided, origami, handmade, vintage books and maps
- **paper alternatives** – printable fabric sheets and shrink plastic. Printable fabric can be used to add photographs or digital designs to your work and comes with a paper backing that stabilizes the fabric for use in an inkjet printer. Shrink plastic sheets also come in inkjet-printable form. These sheets have a matte finish on one side that allows ink to adhere to it and also provides a matte surface on the finished piece.

- **adhesives** – acrylic gel, decoupage medium, foam tape. Acrylic gel is available in different consistencies and finishes. In this book, we will use soft acrylic gel in both matte and gloss finishes. Acrylic gel can also be used as a sealer (see below).
- **paints** – glaze, acrylic, fluid acrylic. Glazes are acrylics thinned with an extender. Fluid acrylics are a pigmented acrylic without the heavy body of a standard acrylic.
- **paintbrushes** – foam, fine, broad
- **rubber stamps** – fine detail, textural, alphabet
- **inks** – pigment, permanent, dye-based
- **gels** and **sealers** – acrylic gel (matte and gloss), Diamond Glaze
- **markers** – permanent, dye-based, detail
- **glitter** – colored, iridescent, German glass glitter, fine
- **cold laminator** – sandwiches delicate paper pieces between two sheets of thin plastic film without using heat. Heat lamination will not work for these projects. I used a Xyron machine, with a laminator cartridge.
- **wax paper** – handy for covering your work top when painting and drying items
- **heat gun** – for drying, embossing, and heating shrink plastic
- **hole punches** – 1/4", 1/8", 1/16"
- **eyelets** and **eyelet-setting tools** – spring loaded, Crop-a-Dile, individual setters

# Inside The Jewelry Studio
## Basic Jewelry Tool Kit

The Basic Jewelry Tool Kit includes tools that most jewelry artists find indispensable. Over time, you might want to add a supply of findings, cords, and lacing to these tools, so that you can readily create new and unique pieces of altered paper jewelry.

Following are the recommended supplies for your Basic Jewelry Tool Kit:

- **wire cutters** – used for cutting wire, head pins, and jump rings. If possible, use flush-cut cutters that create a 90° angle when cutting wire.

- **needle (or flat) nose pliers** – a utilitarian tool used for bending, gripping, and manipulating wire. In jewelry making, it is important to have pliers with a smooth inside. Textured pliers leave marks on your work.

- **round nose pliers** – have a cone-shaped nose made specifically for creating curls and loops in wire

- **crimping pliers** – made for one job only: crimping beads (or tubes). On the inside of these pliers are two notches, one for crimping and one for folding the bead. One of my favorite tools.

- **jump ring pliers** – used to open a double jump ring (also called a split ring). One of the nose ends is bent down, so that you can easily separate the loops. Another of my favorite tools.

Other items to consider:

- **head pins** – plain and decorative, in different lengths and metals. Similar to a sewing pin but without the sharp point. Used to make jewelry components for earrings or dangles.

- **beading needle** – for stringing beads

- **ball chain** – great for quick jewelry pendants and bracelets

- **ready-to-finish jewelry** – watch faces, necklace blanks, bracelet blanks

- **beading string and wire** – stretchable string, cotton string, leather and rubber cord, Tigertail beading wire

- **jewelry findings** – earring posts, ear hooks and wires, pin backs

- **jump rings** – solid, single, double (or split), in different sizes and metals

- **wire** – fine, medium, and thick gauges

- **beads** – seed, crystal, wooden, assorted, metal spacers

- **crimp beads** – small, medium, large, spring end crimps, tubes. Crimp beads and tubes are small metal beads, tubes, or coils used to secure beading string or wire to itself. Crimp beads can also be used to hold a bead in a certain location on a string or wire.

- **clasps** – lobster, toggle, spring, crimp end clasps. Choosing the right clasp for a project is a matter of personal preference and supplies at hand. Large leather cord may require the ruggedness of a crimp end or spring clasp, while a cotton string may require something more delicate such as a toggle clasp. Clasps can be added to a project with jump rings, double jump (or split) rings, or, in the case of a spring clasp and a crimp end clasp, a simple squeeze of the pliers.

## Simple or Eye Loop

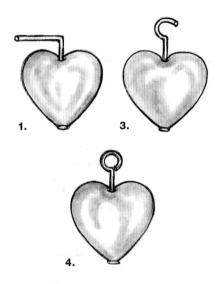

1.

3.

4.

This technique is used many times throughout the book when you need to make an eye or a loop to connect one element to another. You can use either a head pin or a piece of wire to create the simple loop. You will also need a pair of round nose pliers and wire cutters.

1. Use the round nose pliers to bend the wire or head pin to a 90° angle.

2. Cut the bent part of the head to ½" (1.3 cm), if necessary.

3. With the round nose pliers holding the very end of the bent part of the head pin, slowly curl the wire.

4. Continue curling until you have made a circle, releasing and repositioning the pliers, if necessary.

## Double Loop

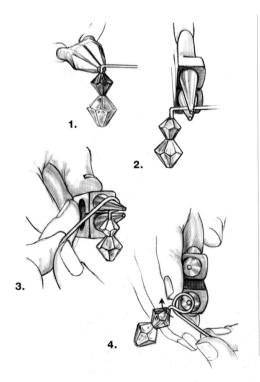

1.

2.

3.

4.

This is a sturdier version of the simple or eye loop and is recommended for jewelry that takes more wear and tear. As with the simple or eye loop, you will need wire or a head pin, round nose pliers, and wire cutters.

1. Use pliers to bend the wire or head pin to a 90° angle.

2. Position the nose of the pliers just past the bend you created.

3. Use your fingers to wrap the head pin around the nose of the pliers to form a loop.

4. Continue to wrap the wire around the nose a second time.

5. Trim the excess wire with the wire cutters.

# Wrapped Loop

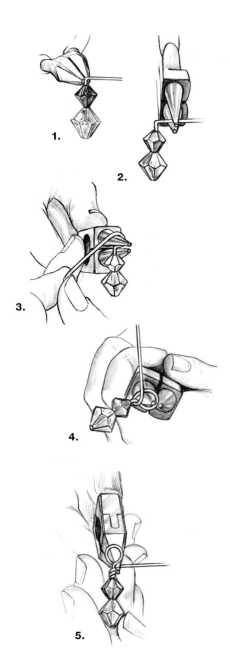

**1.**

**2.**

**3.**

**4.**

**5.**

This loop is a variation of the eye and double loops. It works well for jewelry pieces that are simple but require extra care to keep them secure. You will need a pair of round nose pliers, flat nose pliers, and wire cutters, as well as wire or a head pin.

1. Use round nose pliers to bend the wire or head pin to a 90° angle.

2. Position the nose of the pliers just past the bend you created.

3. Use your fingers to wrap the head pin around the nose of the pliers to form a loop.

4. While gripping the loop tightly with the round nose pliers, use your other hand (if the wire is soft) or a pair of flat nose pliers to wrap the loose head pin end (or wire) around the straight piece of head pin under the loop.

5. Continue to wrap the wire as many times as necessary. Trim as desired and use the flat nose pliers to press the end flat to the straight part of the head pin.

# Opening and Closing Jumps Rings

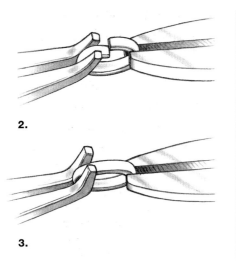

**2.**

**3.**

Follow these easy steps to correctly open and close jump rings and keep their integrity. You will need two pairs of pliers: one flat nose and one round nose.

1. To open a jump ring, start with a pair of pliers in each hand and grasp the ring on both sides of the opening. Open the ring by simultaneously moving one side up and one side down.

2. To close a jump ring, start with a pair of pliers in each hand and grasp the ring on both sides of the opening. Close the ring by simultaneously moving the ends toward each other.

3. When the two ends meet, you might hear a snapping sound, indicating that the ends are flush.

# Overhand Knot and Sliding Closure

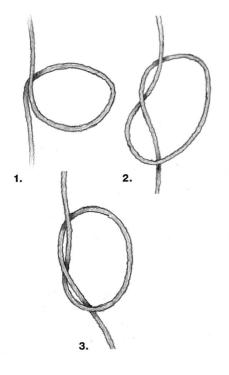

**1.**     **2.**

**3.**

The overhand knot serves as the main element in a sliding closure. To create this knot, you will need string or cord. For the overhand knot:

1. Make a loop with the string or cord.

2. Bring one end of the cord under and through the loop.

3. Pull both ends of the string to tighten the knot.

For the sliding closure:

1. Start to make a knot in one end of the string, as in steps 1 and 2, above.

2. Insert the other end of the string through the loop before pulling the knot tight, creating a looped necklace (or bracelet) shape.

3. Tie the free end of the string that you pulled through the loop in an overhand knot around the already knotted string.

4. The knots should move freely back and forth over the string to adjust the size of the necklace (or bracelet).

# Crimp Bead

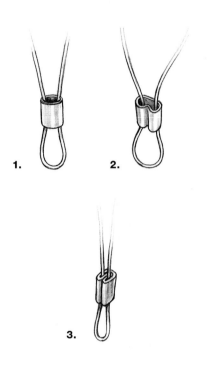

**1.**

**2.**

**3.**

A crimp bead is handy, not only to secure a finding or clasp to the end of a piece of jewelry but also to float beads or embellishments along a length of string, wire, or cord. The illustrations here show crimping at the end of a piece of jewelry, but the crimps are used in the same way on single or double pieces of string, wire, or cord. You will need a crimp bead; string, wire, or cord; and crimping pliers.

1. Slide the end of a length of beading wire through the crimp bead and then create a loop by feeding the end of the wire back into the bead. (If you are attaching a finding, such as a clasp, thread the wire through the clasp before feeding it back through the crimp bead.)

2. Position the crimp bead inside the second notch in the crimping pliers and close the pliers

   around the bead. You should see a groove down the middle of the crimp bead with a wire on each side. (If you are using the crimp bead to float another bead you will have only one wire in the crimp bead.)

3. Position the same crimp bead in the first notch of the crimping pliers and close the pliers, so that you fold the crimp bead in half along the groove created in step 2.

# Spring End Crimp Bead

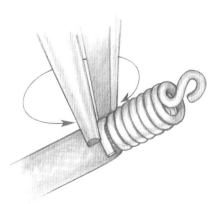

A spring end crimp bead is used when you have a thick cord or a double thickness of string that won't fit through a regular crimp bead. A spring end crimp bead with an extended loop can serve as half a clasp, as well. To finish the clasp, add a spring end crimp bead to the other end of the string and a lobster clasp to the extended loop.

For this technique, you will need flat nose pliers, a spring end crimp bead, and cord or string.

1. Insert the end of the string or cord into the spring end crimp bead but don't go all the way through.

2. Use the flat nose pliers to flatten the first coil of the spring end crimp bead, to lock the string or cord into place.

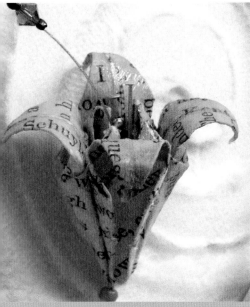

# CHAPTER
## 2

# *Purely Paper*

A MORE APT TITLE FOR THIS CHAPTER MIGHT BE "BEWARE THE PAPER CUT," as we fold, roll, cut, and laminate paper for each of the projects and variations that follow. This section uses paper in its simplest form. By making slight changes to humble pieces of paper, you can make beautiful jewelry.

For example, acrylic glazes are combined with old book pages, which are folded to make elegant origami beads in Lilies of the Neckline (page 20). For its variation, pieces of paper are manipulated and glittered to recreate the lily as the star of a pair of elegant earrings.

By laminating paper in the Mood Swings: Laminated Paper Pendant (page 24), we make it sturdy enough to serve as a changeable pendant or, as in the variation, a unique bracelet.

For the A Trip Remembered necklace project (page 28), we'll collect memories in tiny folded journals that can be hung around your neck. For the key ring variation, we'll create a green grocery list journal that you can clip onto your purse or satchel.

The last project in the chapter will have you seeing clearly. Even if you aren't yet old enough to wear reading glasses, you might appreciate their magnification power when working on a wee beading part of a jewelry project. But why wear boring magnifying glasses, when you can embellish them with a paper-beaded eyeglass chain? Learn how to make it in Looking Good (page 32). While you're at it, whip up some beads for the Striped and Sassy earrings described in the variation project (page 34).

As you read through this chapter, consider how you can alter a project by incorporating your favorite color or coordinating it with a special outfit. Simple adjustments in scale or supplies can personalize your piece of jewelry so specifically that you'll want to wear it all the time. Keep in mind that, like other pieces of art, these jewelry projects can be delicate. Some can accept some abuse; others are better saved for special occasions. Oh, and if you do get a paper cut, just know that gel medium is not *really* supposed to be used to seal the cut.

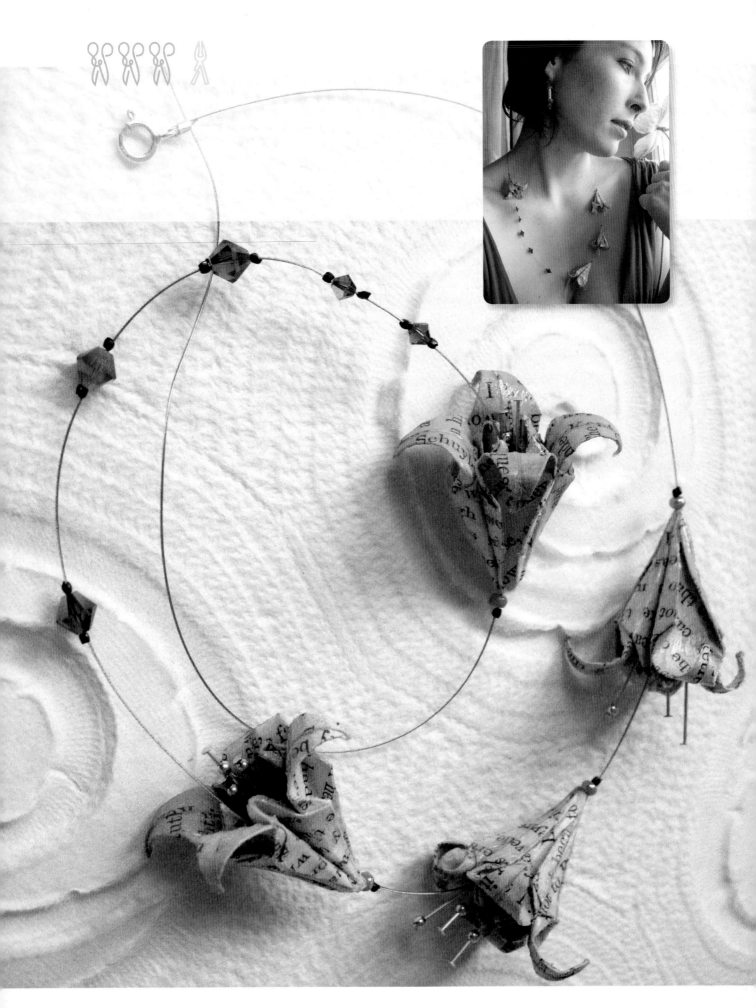

# Lilies of the Neckline:
## Origami Necklace

## Materials

**Basic Paper Tool Kit**

**Basic Jewelry Tool Kit**

**sturdy vintage book pages**

**acrylic glazes (pink, green, and turquoise were used here)**

**paintbrush**

**folding instructions (see appendix, page 121)**

**acrylic gel (gloss)**

**eighteen small black crimps**

**three medium faceted crystal beads (turquoise)**

**two small faceted crystal beads (turquoise)**

**Tigertail beading wire**

**twelve small silver beads**

**twelve 1½" (4 cm) silver head pins**

**eight pink seed beads**

**spring clasp**

**jump ring**

**two silver crimps**

I CAN'T IMAGINE WRITING A BOOK ON ALTERED PAPER JEWELRY without including an origami project. The challenge in creating this necklace was to come up with an origami shape that lends itself to being worn. My daughter is fond of "cootie catchers" (those folded paper fortune tellers), but I wouldn't want to wear them. As I researched origami books and websites, the idea of an airy floral necklace developed. I used an old book as my paper supply, but I made sure that the paper was supple enough to be folded many times. By adding head pins and silver beads, I was able to create a whimsical necklace that is definitely a conversation piece. Adding acrylic gel to the finished folded flowers helps make them sturdier.

1. Cut four 2½" (6.25 cm) squares from the vintage book pages.

2. Apply pink glaze to the center of one side of each of the squares. Let dry.

3. Turn two of the squares over and apply turquoise glaze to the corners and green glaze to the remaining outside edges. Let dry.

4. Turn the other two squares over and apply green glaze to the corners and turquoise glaze to the remaining outside edges. Let dry.

5. Follow the directions on page 121 to fold all four squares into origami lilies.

6. Apply two coats of acrylic gel to each lily, allowing them to dry after each coat.

7. Use an awl to poke a hole in the base of each lily.

8. Use the black **crimp beads** (page 17) to space the three medium and two small faceted beads on the Tigertail, as shown in the photograph.

9. To create the stamens, slide a silver bead onto a head pin and create an **eye loop** (page 14) at the end. Bend the eye so that it is perpendicular to the rest of the head pin. Repeat with all the head pins.

10. To add the flowers to the Tigertail, first add a black crimp, then a pink bead, followed by three of the bent head pins, the flower (opening end first), a second pink bead, and a second black crimp.

11. Repeat with the remaining flowers.

12. Trim the Tigertail to the desired length, then add the spring clasp and jump ring with the silver crimps.

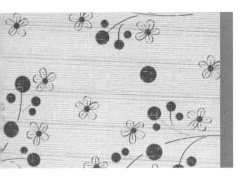

# Glitter Lilies:
## Origami Variation

**Basic Paper Tool Kit**

**Basic Jewelry Tool Kit**

**decorative printed paper**

**ink (pink)**

**folding instructions (see appendix, page 121)**

**paintbrush**

**acrylic gel (gloss)**

**fine transparent glitter**

**silver wire (use a gauge that fits through the bugle beads)**

**forty green frosted bugle beads**

**two silver head pins**

**fourteen pink seed beads**

**two silver ear hooks**

THIS EARRING VARIATION OF THE ORIGAMI LILIES IS ALL ABOUT glimmer. The edges of the paper are lightly colored with ink before the paper is folded, and, as a final touch, the inside of the lily is brushed with gel medium and coated with a fine dusting of glitter. Iridescent seed beads and a leaf made from wire and frosted bugle beads complete the transformation. The result is whimsy and glamour rolled into one.

1. Cut two 2" (5 cm) squares from the decorative paper.

2. Lightly brush the ink pad over the edges of the printed side of the squares.

3. Follow the directions on page 121 to fold both squares into origami lilies.

4. Apply two coats of acrylic gel to both lilies, allowing them to dry after each coat.

5. Apply a thin coat of gel to the inside of the lilies. While the gel is still wet, sprinkle them with glitter. Let dry.

6. Use an awl to poke a hole in the base of the lilies.

7. To create the leaves, cut two 4" (10 cm) pieces of wire and fold them in half. String each half with approximately ten bugle beads and make a **simple loop** (page 14) at each end.

8. Bring the loops together and bend the bugle-covered wire into a leaf shape.

9. On a head pin, string one pink bead, the lily, six more pink beads, and the two loops of the leaf. Close the head pin with a loop.

10. Attach the head pin loops to the ear hooks.

# Mood Swings:
## Laminated Paper Pendant

## Materials

**Basic Paper Tool Kit**

**Basic Jewelry Tool Kit**

**template (page 118)**

**vintage advertisements**

**book text**

**Xyron machine with laminator cartridge**

**ball chain**

**office binder clip**

IF YOU ENJOYED MOOD RINGS AS A CHILD, YOU'LL FALL FOR THIS pendant of personality changes. This great office clip (a binder clip can also be used) holds a series of vintage farmer's almanac ads collaged with fun thoughts that portray some of my different moods: *Mother May I?* (my insecure phase), *I can try* (collaged over a "feeling old" ad, for my days of indecisiveness) and *her heart sparks!* (for those days when I'm feeling smitten).

Laminating this moody ornament (I used the laminator cartridge in my Xyron machine) makes it longer lasting yet light enough to add more moods if I feel inclined. For an even sturdier set of mood collages, you can use 3M's luggage tag laminators. These are harder to cut but are definitely more rigid. The heat seal–type of lamination does not work for this project because you need to cut it right to the edge of the collage and cannot leave a sealed border around it.

So, if the "mood" grabs you, try your hand at one of these.

1. Trace the template onto the chosen advertisement and cut out. Repeat for as many tags as desired.

2. Cut out words from the book text to spell chosen phrases and adhere to the ad tags with a glue stick.

3. Following the manufacturer's instructions, laminate the ad tags.

4. Cut around each tag with scissors.

5. Cut out the hole with a craft knife.

6. String the ball chain through the binder clip and add the tags.

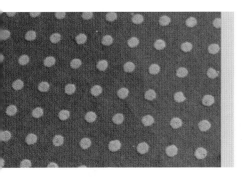

# Wrist Ringlet:
## Laminated Paper Variation

## Materials

**Basic Paper Tool Kit**

**Basic Jewelry Tool Kit**

**template (page 118)**

**double-sided paper**

**Xyron machine with laminator cartridge**

**Crop-a-Dile or other hole punch and setting tool**

**twenty snaps**

**two crimp beads**

**toggle clasp**

**Tigertail beading wire**

**twenty-four pink beads**

FOR THE FRUGAL CRAFTER, ARTIST, OR PAPER LOVER, THERE IS nothing better than the two-for-one goodness of a double-sided sheet of decorative paper. In addition to getting two papers in one sheet—which saves space, so you can buy more paper—it saves money. But what good is two-sided paper if you can't see both sides at once? This laminated paper and snap bracelet variation is the perfect excuse to go rifling through your two-sided paper stash. Go on, show us your back side!

1. Use the template to trace and cut out five bracelet segments from the double-sided paper. Mark the hole placement with a pencil.

2. Following the manufacturer's directions, laminate all five segments.

3. Use the Crop-a-Dile or other punch to punch the marked holes.

4. Fold two of the segment ends to the front and secure with snaps to create the *front segments*.

5. Repeat with the other three segments, showing the reverse side of the paper to create the *reverse segments*.

6. Use a **crimp bead** (page 17) to add the toggle to one end of the Tigertail.

7. String the free end of the Tigertail as follows:

   Four pink beads, reverse segment, one bead, front segment, one bead, reverse segment, one bead, front segment, one bead, reverse segment, four beads.

8. Add the loop half of the clasp and repeat the above stringing pattern along the bottom of the bracelet.

9. Secure the end of the Tigertail to the toggle clasp with a crimp bead.

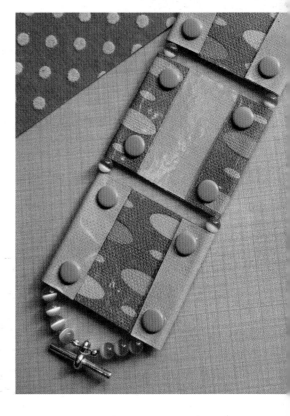

# A Trip Remembered:
## Mini Journal Necklace

## Materials

**Basic Paper Tool Kit**

**Basic Jewelry Tool Kit**

**paintbrush**

**fluid acrylic paints**

**brass frame locket
(approximately 1" × 1½"
[2.5 × 4 cm])**

**black permanent ink**

**colored cotton string**

**bead cap**

**assorted beads**

**two crimp beads**

**toggle clasp**

**template (page 119)**

**vintage map**

**photos (index size)**

**black card stock scrap**

**brass embellishment**

FROM THE FIRST TIME I SAW *ANNIE* ON THE BIG SCREEN, I'VE BEEN in love with lockets. My husband even got me one for Christmas the year our daughter was born and put her picture and a lock of her almost non-existent hair in it! This small locket houses a mini album that is magically cut and folded from one small piece of paper. It is also the perfect size for holding index print–size photographs. The paper used for the journal is actually an old map of Ireland, and the pictures are from a recent trip to the country. Now, doesn't that just make you want to take a trip right now? Or maybe you would like to commemorate a special person, an event, or even a favorite poem. Whatever you choose, keep it close to your heart in one of these necklaces.

### FOR THE LOCKET:

1. Randomly apply acrylic paint to the brass locket frame and let dry.

2. Lightly brush the ink pad over the surface and edges of the locket to distress it.

3. Run a 22" (55 cm) piece of string through the top notch of the brass locket and tie it in an **overhand knot** (page 16). Add a bead cap over the knot.

4. Cut a second piece of string 20" (50 cm) long and string it with 2½" (6.25 cm) of beads.

5. Pair the beaded string and the locket string (you should have two sets of string ends). Use a **crimp bead** (page 17) to attach one set of string ends to the toggle part of the clasp.

6. Repeat with the second set of string ends and the loop part of the clasp.

7. Hold the necklace up. Find the natural point where the two strings meet and tie an overhand knot on each side.

### FOR THE MINI JOURNAL:

1. Use the template (page 119) to size and cut the mini journal from the vintage map.

2. Use the template to fold the journal, then open completely.

3. Decorate the pages with photographs.

4. Start at one end of the piece of paper and fold the journal, like an accordion, to form a book shape

5. Decorate the journal cover with a piece of black card stock, a scrap piece of map, a photograph, and a brass embellishment.

6. Insert the journal into the locket.

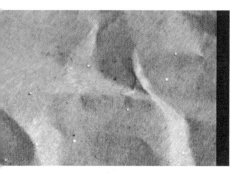

# It's Easy Being Green:
## Mini Journal Variation

## Materials

**Basic Paper Tool Kit**

**Basic Jewelry Tool Kit**

**template (page 120)**

**recycled paper grocery bag**

**round toothpick**

**recycled cardboard packaging**

**brass frame locket**

**key ring finding**

**double jump ring**

I LIKE TO REDUCE MY CARBON FOOTPRINT WHENEVER I CAN, AND it was just after I packed up the recycling when I thought about creating an environmentally friendly shopping-list journal in a refillable keychain holder. Why not recycle the cardboard packaging and paper grocery bags into fun, repurposed journals? Of course, this meant I had to run back outside to gather materials from the recycle bin. After a few cuts of paper bag and the insertion of a toothpick, I had a series of shopping-list journals that I keep attached to my keys.

1. Use the template (page 120) to cut four "pages" from the unprinted section of the paper grocery bag.

2. Stack two pages on top of each other and fold the stack in half. Following the markings on the template, make three small cuts in the spine. Fold the four sections back and forth to create fold lines.

3. Repeat with the second two pages.

4. To create the connecting spine, push in the second and fourth sections of the first two pages, so that the fold is on the inside. Now push in the first and third sections of the second two pages.

5. Lay the first two pages on top of the second two and push the toothpick through all four sections to hold the journal together.

6. Cut the excess toothpick from the top and bottom.

7. Use the cover template (page 120) to cut two covers from recycled cardboard. Adhere them to the front and back of the journal.

8. Insert the journal into the locket.

# Looking Good:
## Paper Bead Eyeglass Chain

## Materials

**Basic Paper Tool Kit**

**Basic Jewelry Tool Kit**

**two-sided decorative paper**

**toothpicks**

**acrylic gel (gloss)**

**wax paper**

**assorted beads**

**eyeglass cord kit**

I ADMIT IT. I LOVE READING GLASSES! I DON'T NEED THEM—YET. But I'm really looking forward to buying a pair to go with every outfit, once I do. As I watch those who do wear reading glasses constantly searching for them, I also see the need for a better-looking eyeglass chain. This chain is made from hip, double-sided, polka dot paper rolled into beads, but it can easily be made from old magazines, newsprint, or vintage book pages. The trick to creating a piece like this without getting bored or going crazy is mass production and a good movie. Cut all your pieces (this chain includes thirty-seven beads), flip on the flick, and start rolling. You'll have to stop every now and then to wash the acrylic gel off your fingers and take a handful of popcorn, but the outcome of a fashionably handy set of reading glasses is worth it.

1. Cut approximately thirty-seven long, narrow triangles of paper, roughly ½" (1.3 cm) wide by 6" (15 cm) long. (You can change the length of your cord by varying the number of beads you use.)

2. Lay a toothpick on the wide end of one triangle and roll the paper tightly around the toothpick. When you have finished rolling the paper, tack the end to the paper bead with acrylic gel and hold it tight for a few seconds, until it adheres. Remove the bead from the toothpick.

3. Repeat with the remaining pieces of paper. If the toothpick gets dirty, replace it with a clean one.

   Note: You can change the shape of the bead by how you roll it. Keeping the skinny point in the center gives you an evenly shaped oblong bead. If you roll it so that one edge stays even, you will get a conically shaped bead.

4. Cover your workspace with wax paper. Dip your thumbs and fore-fingers into the acrylic gel and coat each bead with gel. (You could do this with a paintbrush, but it would be tedious and not as much fun!)

5. Let the beads dry completely.

6. Lay out a pattern with your new paper beads and the other assorted beads and string them onto the kit string.

7. Use the **crimp beads** (page 17) from the kit to adhere the chain to the rubber loops that slip over the eyeglass frames.

# *Striped and Sassy:*
## Paper Bead Variation

## Materials

**Basic Paper Tool Kit**

**Basic Jewelry Tool Kit**

**striped decorative paper**

**toothpicks**

**acrylic gel (gloss)**

**wax paper**

**assorted beads**

**eight decorative head pins**

**two jump rings**

**two ear hooks**

DIFFERENT PAPERS MAKE DIFFERENT BEADS. SOUNDS SIMPLE, BUT until you start rolling, you won't know what your beads will look like. Large prints lose something in a project this small. However, small prints, such as the stripes I used for these beads, add a certain *joie de vivre* to the piece, which can be embellished with fun beads and findings. The whimsy in this pair of earrings is exaggerated by the variations in the bead groupings. For a more austere pair of earlobe ornaments, consider a single-stranded dangle created from a more ornate paper. The possibilities are infinite.

1. Cut four strips measuring ¼" to ½" (6 mm to 1.3 cm) wide and 5" (12.5 cm) long vertically from the striped paper, and four same-size strips horizontally from the striped paper.

2. Lay a toothpick on the end of one of the strips and roll the paper tightly around the toothpick.

3. Tack the end to the bead with acrylic gel and hold it tight for a few seconds, until it adheres. Remove the bead from the toothpick.

4. Repeat with the remaining seven strips of paper.

5. Cover your workspace with wax paper. Dip your thumbs and forefingers into the acrylic gel and coat each bead with gel.

6. Let the beads dry completely.

7. String the paper beads and other assorted beads onto the decorative head pins to create two sets of four decorated head pins.

8. Create a **simple loop** (page 14) at the end of each head pin.

9. Attach one set of four head pins to the **jump ring** (page 16) and attach the jump ring to the ear hook.

10. Repeat with the remaining head pins.

CHAPTER

3

# Collaged and Layered

E TURN UP THE VOLUME IN THIS CHAPTER, ADDING LAYERS UPON PAPER layers to acrylic shapes, wooden beads, and dominoes. Although some people live by the motto "Keep it simple," collage artists wouldn't be caught dead leaving something unembellished. So, if you're a mixed-media lover, this chapter is for you.

As you flip through the following pages, let your mind wander. Unleash your muse and see what new and inspiring techniques you might use to add your special touch to one of these personal adornments. Perhaps you have the perfect text to add to a domino, such as those in the colorful Domino Effect necklace (page 38) or the wear-it-with-anything variation, Mini Mélange (page 40). If you like repetition, you might try repeating yourself with many little collages, as I did in the Asian Adornment: Filled Frames Bracelet (page 42), or you might prefer the simpler but still eye-catching variation, the Digit Decorum ring (page 44).

For a bigger splash, check out the Baubled Bangle (page 46) to see how to wear a party on your wrist. Not to be outdone is the sophisticated variation, Textbook Case (page 48), in which you will find out how you can do more with less.

If you're in the mood to *wrap* it all up, then Kimono-esque Jewel (page 50) is the piece for you; I'll show you how to take a jumbo bead and make it paperlicious. And, in the paper-encased variation, Conquering Cuff (page 52), you'll find out that a good message is worth repeating.

Make sure your acrylic gel supply is optimal and your distractions minimal and get into the groove with these collaged and layered pieces. No matter which project you choose to create, you're sure to make a statement.

"Tick-tock, tick-tock."

# Domino Effect: Game Piece Necklace

## Materials

**Basic Paper Tool Kit**

**Basic Jewelry Tool Kit**

**decorative paper**

**pre-drilled domino**

**paintbrush**

**acrylic gel (matte)**

**vintage text**

**found watch face**

**metal choker necklace**

**one package of small glass beads (millefiore beads were used)**

**fine-gauge brass wire**

IF YOU'RE A FUN-AND-GAMES KIND OF PERSON, THIS PIECE MIGHT appeal to your inner child. I love to hold and stack (and knock over) dominos—but using them as blank canvases for little collages is just as much fun. This necklace plays with bright colors and whimsical additions, such as the watch face and the text that reads "tick tock," but it remains elegant with the addition of the beautiful *millefiore* ("thousand flowers") beads wrapped around the choker.

1. Cut paper to fit the front of the domino. Cut paper for the sides, if desired.

2. Use the paintbrush and acrylic gel to adhere the paper to the domino.

3. Adhere the text and the watch face. Let dry.

4. Thread the domino onto the necklace (remove the screw ball closure to access the necklace wire).

5. Thread half of the beads onto a 20" (51 cm) piece of brass wire.

6. Wrap one end of the brass wire around the first bead to secure the end.

7. Push the remaining beads down against this first bead.

8. Starting at the loose end of the beads, secure the wire by twisting it around the necklace on the right side of the domino. You should now have all of the beads on one side of the wire, leaving the other half of the brass wire empty.

9. Use the empty half of the brass wire to wrap the beaded wire around the necklace. (Wrap the wire tightly around every other bead.)

10. When you get to the end of the wire, you should be at the necklace closure. Twist the end of the wrapping wire around the end of the beaded wire to hold the wire in place.

11. Trim off any excess empty wire and use a pair of pliers to tuck the loose end back into the first bead.

12. Repeat steps 5 through 11 using a second piece of wire and the other half of the beads for the other side of the domino.

# Mini Mélange:
## Game Piece Variation

## Materials

**Basic Paper Tool Kit**

**Basic Jewelry Tool Kit**

**decorative paper
(with fine details)**

**pre-drilled domino**

**letter sticker**

**paintbrush**

**acrylic gel (gloss)**

**rub-ons**

**rhinestone or flat-back
crystal**

**cotton cording**

**two end crimps**

**toggle clasp**

**two jump rings**

TIED ON A COTTON STRING AND SECURED WITH CRIMP ENDS, THIS variation of the game piece collage is even easier than the original. It's especially fun to make with children who can make good use of scraps and stickers. For a child-friendly closure, start with a longer cord and just tie it closed with a knot or use a double knotted **sliding closure** (page 16).

1. Cut paper to fit the front of the domino.

2. Use a paintbrush and acrylic gel to adhere the paper to the domino.

3. Cut out smaller details and collage them onto the first layer. Let dry. Add letter sticker.

4. Add rub-ons.

5. Add more cut-paper details and rub-ons as desired.

6. Use acrylic gel to adhere the rhinestone and seal the front of the domino. Let dry.

7. Thread cotton cording through the domino and tie a knot on each side of the domino.

8. Cut cotton cord to the desired length and add an **end crimp** (page 17) to each side.

9. Attach a toggle clasp with **jump rings** (page 16).

# Asian Adornment:
## Filled Frames Bracelet

## Materials

**Basic Paper Tool Kit**

**Basic Jewelry Tool Kit**

**photograph frame bracelet**

**decorative paper**

WHETHER YOU LOVE OR DESPISE SCRAPBOOKING, YOU CAN BE SURE that as the number of memory keepers increases, so do the number of neat trinkets and products manufactured for these custodians of photography. From this, we all can benefit. These amusing little bracelets, meant to hold portraits of loved ones, are easily adapted to hold miniature collages and works of art. If you can envision your art in Lilliputian scale, you will easily come to love wearing it on a bracelet such as this. For this bracelet, each collage is slightly different, but you could tell one continual story as the bracelet wraps around your wrist, or you might choose to create a story and duplicate it in each frame. Don't forget to pull out your fine-point scissors and your tweezers—this is an up-close and personal endeavor.

1. Remove the clear plastic (and sample photo) from each frame.

2. Using the clear plastic as a template, choose a section of decorative paper to showcase, and trace around the plastic with a pencil.

3. Repeat step 2 for each frame.

4. Cut out the penciled decorative paper pieces.

5. Cut coordinating elements from other areas of the decorative paper (I used a small strip of decorative border to tie all the pieces together) and adhere them with acrylic gel to the main paper pieces.

6. Insert the mini collages into the frames and cover them with the provided clear plastic covers.

# *Digit Decorum:*
## Filled Frames Variation

## Materials

**Basic Paper Tool Kit**

**Basic Jewelry Tool Kit**

**frame from a photograph frame bracelet**

**decorative paper**

**beading needle**

**seed beads**

**stretchable beading string**

CAN IT GET ANY MORE FUN THAN THIS? ONE LITTLE COLLAGE OR piece of art in one frame, on one finger, or one on each finger—you choose. By using stretchable beading string and a collection of coordinating seed beads, you can easily turn a frame cut from a bracelet into a ring that fits any finger size. Of course, by cutting one of the frames from a bracelet, you end up with a handful of leftover blank frames, just begging to become rings for your other fingers. How can you say no?

1. Remove the clear plastic cover (and sample photo) from the frame.

2. Using the clear plastic as a template, choose a section of decorative paper to showcase, and trace around the plastic with a pencil. Cut the piece out.

3. If desired, cut coordinating embellishments from the decorative paper and adhere them with acrylic gel to the main piece.

4. Insert the paper or mini collage into the frame and cover it with the provided clear plastic cover.

5. Use the beading needle to string beads onto a 4" (10 cm) piece of string. (I used thirty-seven beads—adjust the number of beads to fit your finger.)

6. Thread the string through the top hole of one side of the frame and the bottom hole on the other side of the frame, so that the beaded part of the string forms a band. (See photo.)

7. Tie the string in a triple knot behind the frame and trim off the excess.

8. Repeat with a second piece of string and beads and thread them through the other two holes of the frame.

# Baubled Bangle:
## Paper-Covered Bead Bracelet

## Materials

**Basic Paper Tool Kit**

**Basic Jewelry Tool Kit**

**wax paper**

**decorative Japanese paper**

**paintbrush**

**acrylic gel (matte)**

**seven assorted wooden beads**

**large-link antiqued brass chain**

**antiqued brass lobster clasp**

**assorted glass beads**

**antiqued brass head pins**

LOOKING SLIGHTLY LIKE JAPANESE LANTERNS, JOVIAL PAPER-covered beads hang from an oversize-link chain in this bubbly bracelet. The initial inspiration for this bracelet was a retro, large-bead necklace I came across at a flea market. All I needed to do was hippify the basic design to create a smashingly current, must-have bracelet. Small hints of shimmer in the glass beads create a pleasant contrast to the antiqued brass chain and head pins. The colorful beads are softened by a coat of matte acrylic gel, but they could easily be bathed in gloss gel to scream, "Here I am!"

1. Cover your work surface with wax paper.

2. Cut randomly sized narrow strips of decorative paper.

3. Coat the strips of paper with matte gel and adhere them to the wooden beads.

4. Cover the entire bead with matte gel and let dry.

5. If necessary, use pliers to remove rings to size the chain for your wrist. Add a lobster clasp.

6. Create small dangles by stringing three beads onto a head pin and then making a **double loop** (page 14).

7. Create large dangles by stringing two beads, a covered wooden bead, and a third small bead onto a head pin and then making a double loop.

8. Attach the double loop of the large and small dangles to the chain.

# Textbook Case:
## Paper-Covered Bead Variation

## Materials

**Basic Paper Tool Kit**

**Basic Jewelry Tool Kit**

**wax paper**

**vintage script book text**

**paintbrush**

**acrylic gel (gloss)**

**large wooden bead**

**two copper-colored, doughnut-shaped beads**

**black rubber tubing (matte)**

**two end crimps**

**two double jump rings**

**toggle clasp**

A HUNDRED TIMES MORE SUBTLE THAN THE BAUBLED BANGLE, this covered-bead variation is classic in its simplicity. Text from a vintage book is wrapped over, under, and around a wooden bead before being glazed with gloss gel. The shiny bead and its copper-colored counterparts contrast elegantly with the matte rubber tubing used for this uncomplicated necklace. You can wear this piece with just about any outfit—fancy or everyday. Who knew you could say so much with so little effort?

1. Cover your work surface with wax paper.

2. Cut script sections from a vintage book.

3. Coat the strips of paper with gloss gel and adhere them to the wooden bead.

4. Coat the entire bead with gloss gel and let dry.

5. String the wooden bead between the two copper beads onto the rubber tubing.

6. Add an **end crimp** (page 17) to each end of the rubber tubing.

7. Use double **jump rings** (page 16) to add the toggle clasp.

# *Kimono-esque Jewel:*
## Paper-Encased Bead Pendant

## Materials

**Basic Paper Tool Kit**

**Basic Jewelry Tool Kit**

**acrylic gel (gloss)**

**paintbrush**

**decorative paper**

**flat black bead**
**(1" × 1½" [2.5 × 4 cm])**

**18" (46 cm) thin-gauge**
**silver wire**

**yellow seed beads**

**green bead**

**2½" (6 cm) head pin**

**three jump rings**

**black rubber tubing**

**two end crimps**

**lobster clasp**

I ADORE SIMPLE PROJECTS THAT PROVIDE A LOT OF *POW!* THIS LITTLE pendant starts humbly, with a simple, flat, black bead, but ends as an eye-catching adornment. The addition of beautiful decorative papers, silver wire, and just a few beads makes this necklace a quick and fully customizable gift option.

This piece plays with the strong citrus colors in the paper and the stark black background of the bead to create a classic, Asian-inspired look. To make a sure-to-be-treasured gift for a favorite teacher, change the paper to a photocopy of a vintage class photo, use a slightly different shade of seed bead, and add a passage of text from an old school primer.

1. Using the acrylic gel and the paintbrush, adhere a strip of decorative paper horizontally around the flat bead.

2. Add a second strip of paper vertically to the front of the bead.

3. Brush acrylic gel over the surface of both papers to seal them. Let dry.

4. Wrap the silver wire around the bead, adding the yellow seed beads every couple of wraps, so that they sit on the front of the bead.

5. Twist the wire ends together at the back and trim the excess with needle nose pliers. Tuck the twisted end under the wrapped wire.

6. Thread the green bead onto the head pin and then add the black decorated bead.

7. Use round nose pliers to make an **eye loop** (page 14) at the top of the head pin and insert a **jump ring** (page 16).

8. Thread the black rubber tubing through the jump ring.

9. Add the **end crimps** (page 17) to the ends of the black tubing and secure with needle nose pliers.

10. Add a jump ring to both sides and a lobster clasp to one of the jump rings.

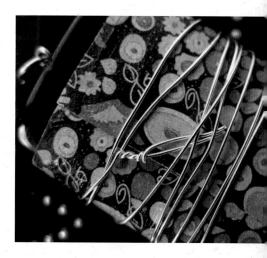

# Conquering Cuff:
## Paper-Encased Variation

## Materials

**Basic Paper Tool Kit**

**Basic Jewelry Tool Kit**

**decorative paper**

**vintage book text**

**ready-to-wear segmented bracelet**

**acrylic gel (matte)**

**paintbrush**

THIS UNIQUE WRIST TRIMMING FEATURES PAPER ENCASING EACH of the individual sections of a ready-made bracelet. Covering a ready-to-wear bracelet with vintage book text and strips of fine Japanese paper transforms it into a personal statement. For this bracelet, I chose to repeat a chapter heading on each piece and cut duplicates from the top of each page of that chapter. Other options include using a story, poem, or even words to a song. The hardest part of this project is finding a good bracelet at the store to personalize. I highly recommend the sale bins at department stores—you never know what kind of stash awaits you.

1. Cut one narrow strip of decorative paper and one small strip of text (I used the chapter header, so that I could repeat the same phrase) for each bracelet segment.

2. Adhere the paper strips to the bracelet with the matte gel and let dry completely.

3. Use a craft knife or scissors to trim any excess from the edges of the bracelet segments.

4. Seal the front and edges of each segment with a coat of matte gel.

CHAPTER

4

# Alluringly Transparent

THIS CHAPTER IS FOR THE PERSON WHO LOVES GLASS-BOTTOM BOAT TOURS, creating assemblages under cloches, and looking at Christmas window displays. This is the see-through chapter, in which we'll combine paper with acrylic shapes, vintage chandelier crystals, resin, and even clear tubing. There is definitely something magical about seeing your artwork under a shiny surface—like framing it under glass.

We start out slowly, with All Buckled Up (page 56), a simple foray into decoupage and acrylic jewelry, then carry on swimmingly, with the Daily Catch variation (page 58). Here, I varied the supplies and slightly altered the techniques, to create a completely different bracelet.

We move from decoupage to full-out collage in the Gorgeous Geisha pendant (page 60), which shows you how much fun it is to layer on *both* sides of the acrylic shape. Keeping up the pace, the Maps and Such variation (page 62) uses smaller acrylic disks to make amazingly simple yet striking earrings and a pendant.

The true bling in this book comes courtesy of the Suspended Sparkler necklace (page 64) and its variation, Chandelier Chic earrings (page 66), in which vintage chandelier crystals are repurposed for a glamorous result.

Rose-Colored Readers (page 68) begs you to alter your reading or sunglasses with paper and resin, while the Buckle, Buckle resin-covered belt (page 70) begs the question—is a belt simply utilitarian or a hip accessory?

Not to be outdone, the Paper Bling necklace (page 72) will have your friends guessing what materials you used. They won't believe they came from the plumbing section of the hardware store. The Marbled Ensemble (page 74) won't convince them, either, but it's so simple to make, you can create one for each of the skeptics.

After trying one or two projects in this chapter, I dare you to pick a favorite. With all the variations and possibilities in these transparent ideas, you could be seeing clearly for quite a while.

# All Buckled Up:
## Acrylic Decoupage Bracelet

## Materials

**Basic Paper Tool Kit**

**Basic Jewelry Tool Kit**

**paintbrush**

**acrylic gel (gloss)**

**five 1½" (4 cm) acrylic buckle embellishments**

**decorative paper**

**12" (30 cm) ribbon**

**magnetic clasp**

**six mini eyelets and eyelet setting tools**

**clear nail polish**

**1" (2.5 cm) piece of wire**

**small bead and charm**

IF YOU JUST LOVE A PARTICULAR DECORATIVE OR VINTAGE PAPER, there is no better way to showcase it than to put it under glass—or acrylic, as the case may be. Simplicity can be a beautiful thing. This bracelet shows off a collection of graphic origami papers, but you could easily use sheet music, Italian printed papers, or even a map from a favorite summer vacation. Once you've mastered this project, be sure to try the acrylic collages that follow, for even more see-through fun.

1. Using a paintbrush, spread acrylic gel on the back of the buckles and adhere them to the paper. Let dry.

2. Cut out around the buckle and through the slots using a craft knife and cutting mat.

3. Lace the ribbon through the buckles to create the bracelet.

4. Thread one end of the ribbon through one side of the magnetic clasp and fold it to the back.

5. Secure the ribbon with three mini eyelets. To do this, poke holes in the ribbon with an awl and set the eyelets using eyelet-setting tools.

6. Trim off the excess ribbon and seal the raw edge of the ribbon with clear nail polish.

7. Repeat for the other side, making sure that the clasp closes properly.

8. To create the charm dangle, use needle nose pliers to create an **eye loop** (page 14) at one end of the wire piece.

9. Add a small bead and make a second eye loop at the end to attach a small charm.

10. Use the first eye loop to connect the dangle to the magnetic clasp.

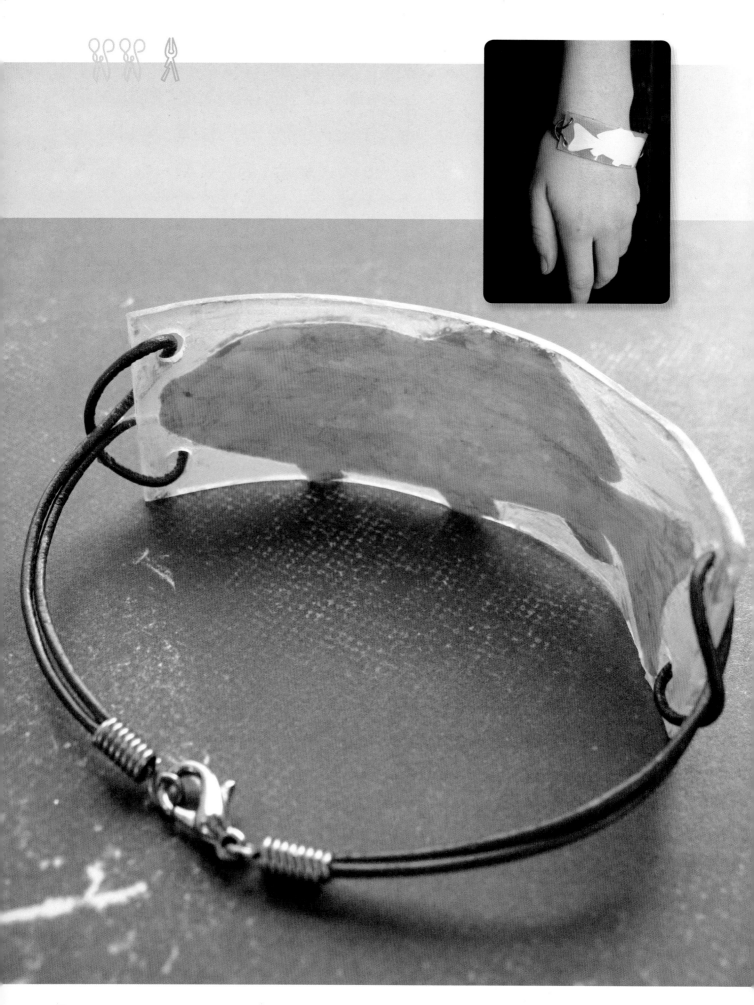

# *Daily Catch:*
## Acrylic Decoupage Variation

## Materials

**Basic Paper Tool Kit**

**Basic Jewelry Tool Kit**

**1" × 3½" (2.5 × 8.75 cm) acrylic label holder with four corner holes**

**heat gun**

**die-cut paper shape (I used a fish)**

**acrylic gel (gloss and matte)**

**fluid acrylic paints**

**copper cording**

**two spring end crimp beads**

**lobster clasp**

WHEN I FOUND THIS PIECE OF ACRYLIC, I IMMEDIATELY WANTED TO turn it into a mixed-media ID bracelet. A little experimenting proved that I could add a slight curve to my piece and make it even more wrist-friendly. The fish is a cut and embossed shape that I purchased on a whim at one of my favorite paper stores, but those of you with seafood aversions can easily replace it with any punched or cut design. The back of the piece was decoupaged with tinted matte acrylic gel to give it a frosted and finished look.

1. While holding the two ends of the acrylic piece to create a slight bow, heat the piece carefully with the heat gun. When the piece starts to bend, remove the heat gun and finish shaping it with your hands. Repeat, if necessary, to get the right shape.

2. Coat the top of the die-cut shape with gloss acrylic gel and adhere it to the back of the acrylic piece.

3. Let dry, then trim off any overhang with a sharp craft knife.

4. Coat the back of the acrylic shape with matte acrylic gel, being sure to seal the edges of the paper.

5. While the gel is still wet, swirl in small amounts of fluid acrylic paint to create a watercolor effect. Let dry.

6. Cut two 6" (15 cm) lengths of the copper cording. Fold one cord gently in half and insert the ends into the holes on the right-hand side of the acrylic piece, creating a loop. Bring the ends back through the loop, pull tight, and secure the ends with a **spring end crimp bead** (page 17).

7. Repeat with the other side.

8. Add a lobster clasp to one of the spring end crimp loops.

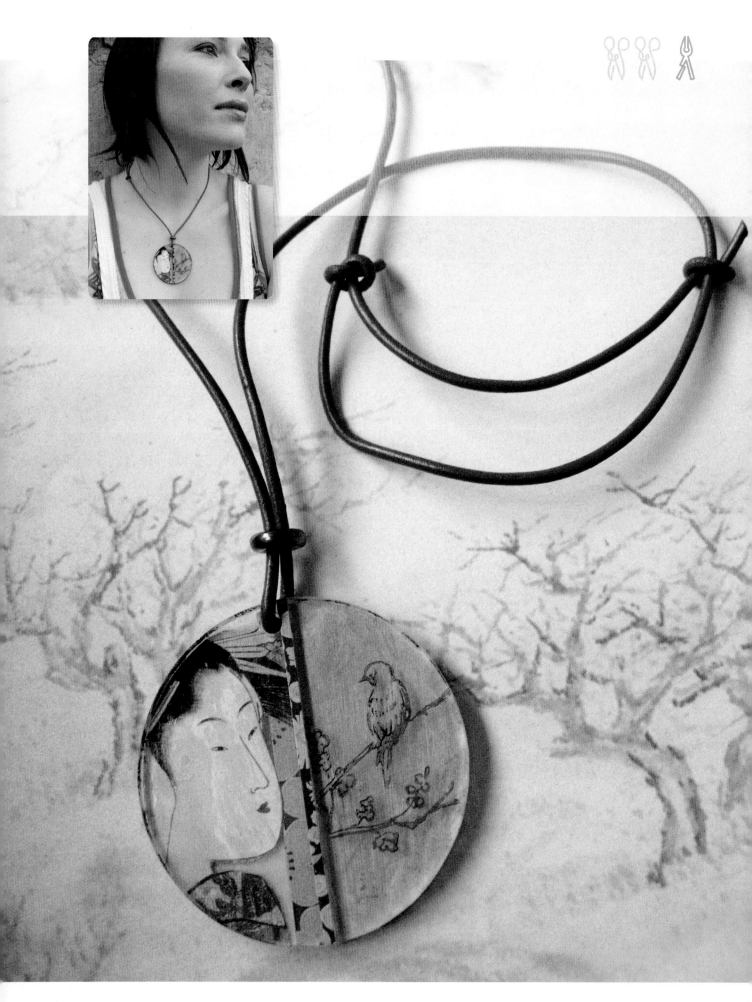

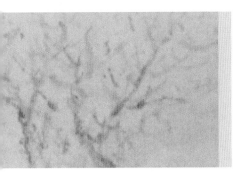

# Gorgeous Geisha:
## Acrylic Collage Pendant

## Materials

**Basic Paper Tool Kit**

**Basic Jewelry Tool Kit**

**Asian scene stamp**

**black and turquoise permanent markers**

**2" (5 cm) acrylic circle**

**decorative Asian-inspired scrapbook paper**

**acrylic gel (matte and gloss)**

**Asian lettering stamp**

**leather cording**

**black circular bead**

ACRYLIC DISKS, SUCH AS THE ONE FEATURED IN THIS PIECE, ARE fun to use because you can easily add dimension to the jewelry by applying elements to both the front and the back of the disk. I like using permanent markers to color rubber stamps for these pieces, because I can single out specific parts of the stamp image—which can be difficult to do with an ink pad. By playing with matte and gloss acrylic gels, you can make different sections of the piece shiny or frosted. When creating your own designs, don't forget the edges of the disk. You can stamp them, like I did on this piece, or you can color them, cover them with paper, or draw on them with the permanent markers. Whatever you choose to do, be sure to seal the paper sections of the collage with acrylic gel, to keep your acrylic collages safe.

1. Color the desired section of the Asian scene stamp with permanent marker and quickly stamp onto the back of the acrylic circle. Repeat as desired with any remaining sections of the stamp.

2. Cut a thin strip of paper and adhere it down the middle of the front of the acrylic circle with matte gel.

3. Cut out the geisha (or other detail) with detail scissors and adhere the image to the back of the circle with gloss gel.

4. Cut out a half circle from paper and adhere it to one half of the back with gloss gel.

5. Stamp the edge of the disk with the Asian lettering stamp and black permanent marker.

6. Paint the remainder of the back of the acrylic circle with matte gel to create a translucent look to the clear sections of the acrylic circle. Let the circle dry.

7. Thread the leather cording through the acrylic circle and then through a black circular bead.

8. Tie a knot in both ends around the cord to create a **sliding closure** (page 16).

# Maps and Such:
## Acrylic Collage Variation

## Materials

**Basic Paper Tool Kit**

**Basic Jewelry Tool Kit**

**paintbrush**

**acrylic gel (gloss)**

**old map**

**texture stamp**

**permanent ink pad**

**rub-ons**

### FOR THE EARRINGS

**two ¾" (2 cm) acrylic circles with hole**

**two 1" (2.5 cm) head pins**

**two crystal beads**

**pair of earring studs with loop**

### FOR THE PENDANT

**one 1¼" (3 cm) acrylic circle with hole**

**charm**

**thin leather cord**

**toggle clasp**

**two silver crimp beads**

I LOVE THE IDEA OF USING A MAP ON THE BACK OF SOMETHING clear, like these acrylic disks. This variation uses a different technique from the one we used in the previous project—we're adhering the entire disk to a background and collaging it from the front. It also shows two other ways to turn the disk into jewelry. Like the previous acrylic decoupage projects, this pendant and earrings are quick and easy to make. The project does call for a few more steps, but these pieces are worth it—you will be complimented every time you wear them.

### FOR THE EARRINGS:

1. Brush acrylic gel on the back of the circles. Adhere the circles to the map. Let dry.

2. Use scissors or a craft knife and cutting mat to trim the excess paper from around the circles.

3. Stamp the texture image with permanent ink onto the front circle and add rub-ons.

4. Seal the front and back of the circles with acrylic gel. Let dry.

5. Cut the head from the head pins with wire cutters.

6. Use round nose pliers to create a large **eye loop** (page 14) in one of the head pins. Insert one of the acrylic circles into this eye.

7. Add a crystal bead, make a small eye at the top of the head pin, and insert the loop of the earring stud into the eye.

8. Repeat steps 7 and 8 with the second acrylic circle.

### FOR THE PENDANT:

1. Use a paintbrush to spread acrylic gel over the back of the circle. Adhere the circle to the map. Let dry.

2. Use scissors or a craft knife and cutting mat to cut the excess paper from around the circle.

3. Stamp the texture image with permanent ink onto the edge of the acrylic circle and add rub-ons to the front.

4. Seal the back and front of the circle with acrylic gel where desired. Let dry.

5. Set the charm over the hole of the acrylic circle and feed the center of the leather cord up through both holes to create a small loop.

6. Feed the ends of the leather cord through the loop and pull tight.

7. Cut the ends of the leather cord to the desired length and add the toggle clasp with the silver **crimp beads** (page 17).

# Suspended Sparkler:
## Crystal Collage Necklace

## Materials

**Basic Paper Tool Kit**

**Basic Jewelry Tool Kit**

**digital photograph**

**inkjet transparency**

**fine paintbrush**

**absorbent ground (white)
(I used Golden)**

**2" (5 cm) green vintage
crystal (with flat back)**

**acrylic gel (gloss)**

**vintage book text**

**gold foiling kit**

**18-gauge silver wire**

**silver necklace kit**

NOTHING MAKES YOU FEEL QUITE AS GLAMOROUS AS WEARING CRYSTAL above your décolletage. Heck, it even works over a T-shirt. This necklace was made by collaging, foiling, and attaching a vintage chandelier crystal to a ready-to-finish necklace from the jewelry aisle of the craft store. Using a colored crystal creates a subtle piece, a result easily reversible by using a clear crystal. The shape and the size of the crystal are also changeable. As long as the back of the crystal is flat, the piece can be decoupaged success-fully. And, if you're just too impatient to wait for your Great Aunt Penny to perish and leave you her crystal chandelier, you can use brand-new crystals. Find them at your local lighting showroom.

1. Print the photograph on an inkjet transparency. The photograph will be reversed in the final project, so reverse it using image-editing soft-ware, if necessary, before printing.

2. Trace the shape of the crystal onto the transparency. (I used an awl to scratch the line.)

3. Cut out the shape and, if necessary, trim it with scissors to fit.

4. Carefully paint absorbent ground over the printed side of the trans-parency. The ground will make the painted areas opaque. For an ethereal look, leave some details unpainted.

5. Adhere the smooth side of the transparency to the crystal with acrylic gel. Let dry.

6. Place the crystal over the vintage text to help you decide which part of the text you'd like to have show through. Trace the section and cut it out.

7. Apply acrylic gel to the front of the text section and quickly and carefully adhere it to the back of the crystal. (Any sudden movement can make the transparency bleed.)

8. Following the manufacturer's direc-tions, apply foiling adhesive and foil to the back of the crystal.

9. Seal the foil with a coat of acrylic gel.

10. Make a small, flat **loop** (page 14) at the end of a 2.5" (6 cm) piece of silver wire. Bend the loop perpen-dicular to the wire and insert the wire through the hole in the crystal, from front to back.

11. Bend the wire at the back of the crystal and make a **wrapped loop** (page 15).

12. String the crystal onto an assembled silver necklace.

# Chandelier Chic:
## Crystal Collage Variation

## Materials

**Basic Paper Tool Kit**

**Basic Jewelry Tool Kit**

**rubber stamp**

**paper**

**permanent black ink**

**two 1½" (4 cm) clear vintage crystals**

**transparency scrapbook embellishment**

**acrylic gel (gloss)**

**gold or silver foiling kit**

**two silver head pins**

**two light blue crystals**

**two silver ear hooks**

I HIT THE JACKPOT ON MY LAST TRIP TO THE ANNUAL LOCAL ANTIQUE fair, where I stumbled upon these small chandelier crystals. Finally! The perfect size crystals for my ears. You'll want to minimize the weight of these little earlobe embellishments as much as possible, so think diminutive when decorating them. I used a light blue Swarovski crystal to accent my darling dangles and a simple head pin to hold them together.

1. Stamp a piece of paper twice with the ink.

2. Place the crystal over the stamped paper section you want to use, trace it, and cut out the shape. Repeat with the second crystal.

3. Decorate each of the stamped papers with a transparent scrapbook embellishment. Trim, if necessary, and adhere the transparencies to the papers with acrylic gel.

4. Adhere the decorated stamped papers to the back of the crystals with acrylic gel.

5. Following the manufacturer's directions, apply foiling adhesive and foil to the back of the crystals.

6. Seal the foil with a coat of acrylic gel.

7. Insert a head pin through the hole in one of the crystals, front to back. Bend the head pin up at the back of the crystal. Push the head pin toward the back of the crystal, to create a slight bend, and add the small blue crystal.

8. Finish the head pin with a **simple loop** (page 14) and attach it to the ear hook.

9. Repeat steps 7 and 8 with the second crystal.

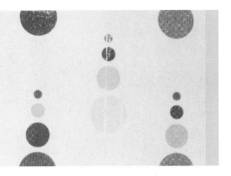

# Rose-Colored Readers:
## Resin Reading Glasses

## Materials

**Basic Paper Tool Kit**

**Basic Jewelry Tool Kit**

**eyeglass repair kit or micro screwdriver**

**reading or sunglasses**

**decorative paper**

**paintbrush**

**acrylic gel (gloss)**

**wax paper**

**cardboard for propping**

**resin kit**

**bamboo skewers or toothpicks**

CAN YOU DIG THESE HIP READING GLASSES? I LOVE THE SHAPE, AND I love that I got them for next to nothing at the local discount department-store sale bin. At that price, I could definitely afford to make a customized pair for all my farsighted friends. And, though I chose to do this with reading glasses, there is no reason you couldn't "pimp" your sunglasses instead. As long as you can remove the sides of the glasses (the part that goes over your ears), you can use this technique. Because the resin is a bit of a sticky, slow process, I recommend doing at least two or even three pairs at a time. At such a low price, they won't break the bank.

1. Using an eyeglass repair kit, remove the screws from the eyeglass ear pieces.

2. Trace the ear pieces onto the back of the decorative paper and cut out the pieces.

3. Trim the decorative paper, if necessary, then use the paintbrush and gel to adhere it to the outside of each ear piece. Add other layers of cut flowers or other paper details.

4. Seal the papers with gel and let it dry completely

5. Place the ear pieces over wax paper and prop them up, if necessary, with cardboard.

6. Follow the manufacturer's directions for mixing the resin, then pour it slowly over the ear pieces. Use the bamboo skewers to make any adjustments in the resin or to remove any drips once the resin has been poured. Make sure the resin does not drip into the screw holes on the sides.

7. When the resin has fully dried, screw the ear pieces back onto the eyeglasses frames.

# Buckle, Buckle:
## Resin Variation

## Materials

**Basic Paper Tool Kit**

**Basic Jewelry Tool Kit**

**buckle**

**vintage dictionary page or decorative paper**

**acrylic gel (gloss)**

**wax paper**

**cardboard for propping**

**resin kit**

**bamboo skewers or toothpicks**

**leather belt kit**

THIS PROJECT IS CALLED BUCKLE, BUCKLE BECAUSE THE VINTAGE text used to cover the buckle (which you can find in the accessories aisle of the fabric store) is the definition of *buckle* from a vintage dictionary. I'm sure your mind is already racing with different cover options, but here are a few more: Chinese text from a Chinese newspaper, the stock exchange (for a Wall Streeter), comic books, magazine advertisements, or just about any gorgeous decorative paper on the market. For the belt itself, I found just what I needed in the leather section of the craft store, but you can also use a strong, wide grosgrain ribbon and a few well-placed small grommets for a lighter belt. It's a cinch.

1. Trace the buckle onto the back of the dictionary page or decorative paper and cut out around the shape, leaving about a ½" (1.3 cm) border to wrap around the buckle.

2. Apply acrylic gel to the top of the buckle and gently lay the cut paper on top.

3. Use scissors or a craft knife to make cuts in the excess paper so that it can be wrapped around to the back of the buckle.

4. Use the acrylic gel to glue the excess paper to the back of the buckle.

5. Seal the entire paper-covered area with a layer of gel.

6. Place the buckle over wax paper and prop it up, if necessary, with cardboard.

7. Follow the manufacturer's directions for mixing the resin, then pour it slowly over the buckle. Use the bamboo skewers to make any adjustments once the resin has been poured.

8. When the resin has fully dried, use the leather belt kit to finish the belt.

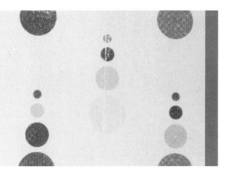

# Paper Bling:
## Plastic Tube Necklace

## Materials

**Basic Paper Tool Kit**

**Basic Jewelry Tool Kit**

**12" (30.5 cm) of 5/16" (8 mm) clear plastic tubing**

**decorative paper (marbled was used)**

**thin paintbrush handle or bamboo skewer**

**thirty-eight faceted beads (two different colors)**

**nineteen 1¼" (3 cm) head pins**

**nineteen 3/8" (1 cm) jump rings**

**purchased chain with large links**

WHO WOULD HAVE THOUGHT YOU COULD MAKE SUCH AN INTERESTING piece of jewelry with plastic tubing? This piece slowly morphed into a necklace after I first played with using the plastic tubing as a handle for an altered cigar box purse. Although the tubing isn't very expensive, you have to buy a roll of it. The remainder of my roll had been sitting in my "cupboard of interesting things" for a while before I thought to pull it out and make beads with it. I find it easier to make a longer bead than I need and cut it down to length. To fill the tube with the paper, use the smallest paintbrush handle or bamboo skewer you can find to roll up the paper. The skinnier you make the tube, the easier your job will be.

For this project and the variation, marbled paper was used, but you can change the whole feel of the piece by changing the paper. The smaller the detail on the paper, the easier it is to make out the design.

1. With scissors, cut four 2½" pieces of the plastic tubing.

2. Use scissors to cut four strips of decorative paper about 2½" × ½" (6 × 4 cm). With the wide edge at the bottom and the short ends at the sides, roll each strip around the paintbrush handle into a long, skinny tube.

3. Slide the paper into the tubes, then use scissors to cut the tubes into ½" (4 cm) pieces. (Make nineteen of these paper-filled tubes.)

4. To create the tube beads, thread a faceted bead onto a head pin, add the paper-filled tube, and then another bead. Secure the pieces by making an **eye loop** (page 14) at the end. Repeat with all the tubes.

5. With pliers, use **jump rings** (page 16) to attach the tube beads to the chain. Start by attaching one at the center of the necklace, then skip a link on either side and attach more tube beads, alternating colors.

6. Continue with the rest of the beads, gradually skipping more and more links between beads, as desired.

# Marbled Ensemble:
## Plastic Tube Variation

USE THE SAME SKILLS YOU LEARNED IN THE PAPER BLING NECKLACE to create this choker and earrings. Instead of using faceted beads for the tops and bottoms of the tubes, try metal bead caps. In place of chain, I've used thin rubber cord, but you could also substitute a leather cord or even waxed twine. The earrings also use bead caps, a couple of beads, and spacers to create a quick and easy project.

## Materials

**Basic Paper Tool Kit**

**Basic Jewelry Tool Kit**

5" (12.5 cm) of ⁵/₁₆" (8 mm) plastic tubing

decorative paper

**thin rubber cord (I used black)**

**six bead caps (two for necklace, four for earrings)**

**two end crimps**

**two silver 2" (5 cm) head pins**

**two faceted beads**

**two silver spacer rings**

**two silver earring hooks**

### FOR THE CHOKER:

1. Use scissors to cut a 2¾" (7 cm) piece of tubing.

2. Cut a piece of decorative paper ½" wide × 2¾" long (4 × 7 cm) and roll into a long, skinny tube. Insert the rolled paper into the plastic tubing.

3. String the tube bead onto the rubber cord and add a bead cap on each side.

4. Tie a knot on the outside of the bead caps to secure.

5. Secure the ends of the cord with **end crimps** (page 17).

### FOR THE EARRINGS:

1. Use scissors to cut a 1½" (4 cm) piece of tubing.

2. Cut a strip of decorative paper ½" wide × 1½" long (1.6 cm × 4 cm) and roll into a long, skinny tube. Insert the paper into the plastic tubing.

3. Cut the tube into two pieces.

4. Create the earrings by threading the head pins as follows: faceted bead, silver spacer ring, bead cap (face up), plastic tube, bead cap (face down).

5. Use round nose pliers to create an **eye loop** (page 14) at the top of the bead (cut off excess head pin, if necessary).

6. Add an earring hook through the eye on the top of the bead and pinch with needle nose pliers to secure.

CHAPTER

5

# Almost Paper

IS THERE A REBEL INSIDE YOU JUST WAITING TO GET OUT? DO YOU LIKE TO THINK outside the box even when you're supposed to be working inside the box? If so, this is your chapter. On the next few pages we'll take a look at things that are "almost paper." First, we'll play with sheets of *plastic* paper, also known, from your childhood days, as shrink plastic. Nowadays, you can even put specially coated shrink plastic through the inkjet printer! Next, we'll play with paper gone wild—a.k.a. paper clay. Once you've molded, pressed, shaped, and let it dry, you can treat it just like you would paper: stamp, glaze, or distress it. Finally, to wrap up the chapter, we'll dabble in the world of *fabric* paper. This is also made to go through the printer, and you can stamp, paint, sew, color, quilt, and embellish it, too.

Try your hand at making Finger Rapt: Shrink Plastic Ring (page 78). It's a good thing you have ten fingers, because you may just want to make that many! If you like to think bigger, try the Ruffled Cuff variation (page 80). Get your fingers dirty tinting paper clay in Rolled and Pressed (page 82), or make time for the Wristful Thinking watch variation (page 84). If fabric appeals to your softer side, then take a look at the hip and nifty Rebel with a Cuff cuff-let (page 86). And you might find that the London Neckline: Fabric Paper variation (page 88) is reason enough to take a trip (for the photograph you'll use, of course).

Keep thinking beyond the expected, go where the paper takes you, and enjoy the scenery in this new world of almost paper.

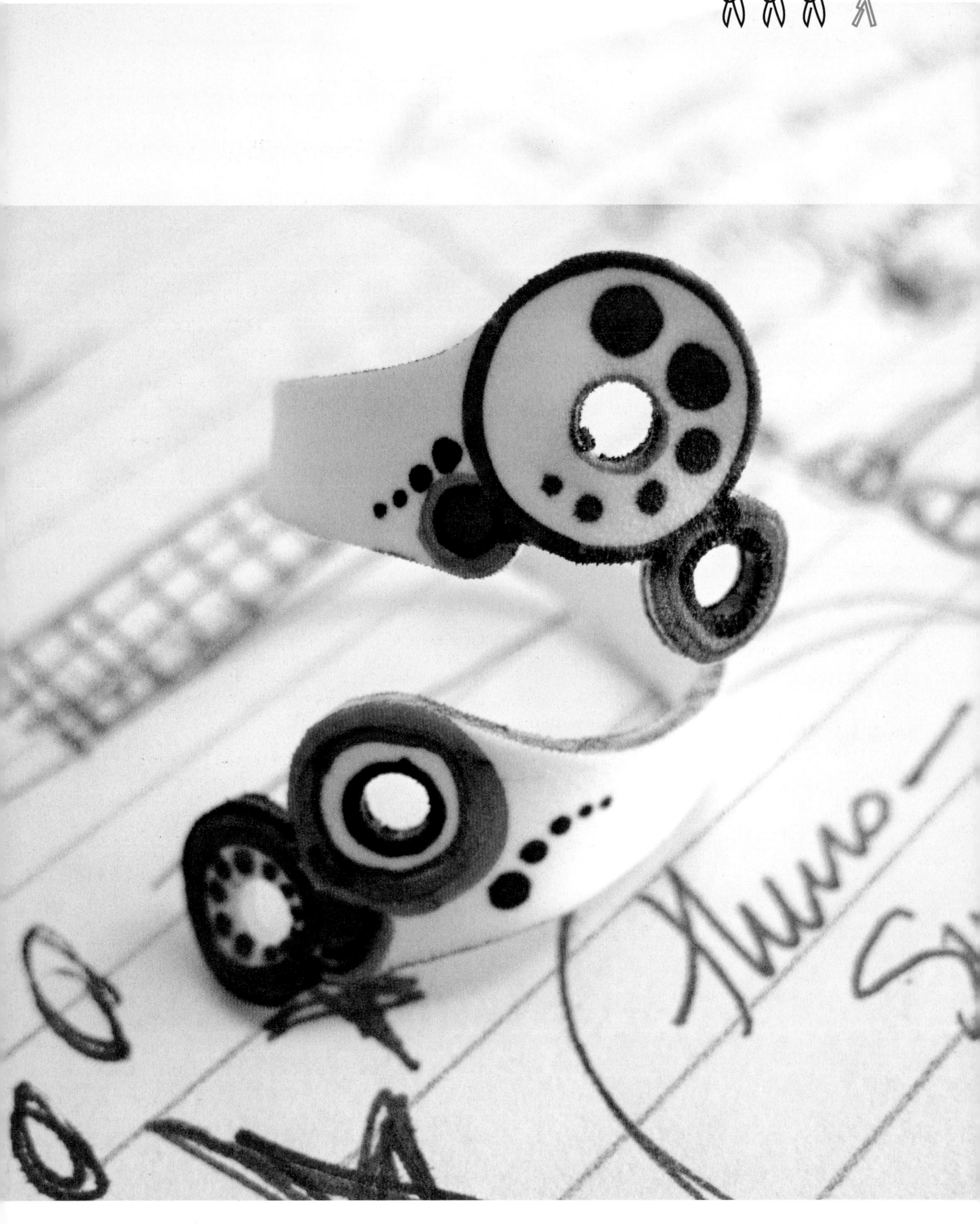

## Finger Rart:
### Shrink Plastic Ring

## Materials

**Basic Paper Tool Kit**

**Basic Jewelry Tool Kit**

**template (page 120)**

**inkjet-printable white shrink plastic (or sanded white shrink plastic)**

**hole punch**

**permanent markers**

**box (shoebox size)**

**heat gun**

**flat object (such as the back of a rubber stamp)**

**craft tweezers and hot pad**

**large dowel or paintbrush handle (about the diameter of your finger)**

YOU REMEMBER SHRINK PLASTIC, DON'T YOU? CHANCES ARE, YOU GOT a kit for your seventh or eighth birthday. The sheets were preprinted with butterflies or horses and came with five colored pencils. Well, the shrink plastic of the twenty-first century comes in clear, translucent, white, and black and is even available in inkjet-printable form (the kind I used).

Because I work with my hands and do a lot of teaching and demos, I love to wear rings. I have rings of all different sizes, to fit all of my fingers. The great thing about this ring is that you don't have to invest in a lot of fancy metal-smithing equipment to make one. Technically, you don't even need a heat gun if you use your oven to melt the piece (but it's not as much fun).

1. Draw your design (or use the template on page 120) onto the shrink plastic and cut it out.

2. Punch holes into the plastic to create see-through sections in the design.

3. Color the shrink plastic with permanent markers. To give the ring a colored edge, run a marker around the edges of the plastic before shrinking it.

4. Place the colored shrink plastic in the shoebox and heat it slowly with the heat gun. It will curl up as it shrinks.

5. When the plastic flattens out, it is fully shrunk. To make it completely flat, for a smooth ring, press it with a flat object, such as the back of a rubber stamp, before it completely cools.

6. Reheat the ring fully, until the plastic is limp. Working quickly, gently pick up the ring with the tweezers, lay the ring over the dowel, and wrap it around using the hot pad. You will probably need to reheat different sections to get the ring to fully wrap around the dowel. The plastic will be hot, so use caution, tweezers, and the hot pad while wrapping the ring.

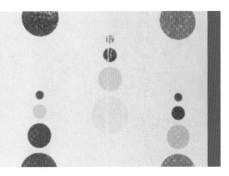

# Ruffled Cuff:
## Shrink Plastic Variation

## Materials

**Basic Paper Tool Kit**

**Basic Jewelry Tool Kit**

**inkjet-printable white shrink plastic (or sanded white shrink plastic)**

**permanent markers**

**rubber stamps and permanent ink (I used StāzOn)**

**box (large shoebox size)**

**heat gun**

**flat object (such as the back of a rubber stamp)**

**craft tweezers and hot pad**

**round bottle or object about the size of your wrist**

**paintbrush**

**pearl mica flake (small) (I used Golden)**

THIS PROJECT IS FOR THE PERSON WHO LIKES TO EXPERIMENT—the trailblazer, the curious sort—because with this project, we are breaking the rules. Typically, when you make anything with shrink plastic, you melt it down to size, then put something big and flat over it to smooth it out. Not us! When our shape is shrunk, we're going to pick it up (with tweezers or a hot pad, because it's going to be *hot*), and we're going to shape and ruffle it. You will probably need to heat it a number of times, especially in isolated spots, to exaggerate the ruffle of the bracelet. This leaves a lot of room, not only for fixing mistakes but also for extreme personalization.

1. Because the plastic shrinks so much, to get a large enough piece for the bracelet, you will need to cut a diagonal strip about 2½" to 3" (6 to 7.5 cm) wide, from one corner of the sheet to the opposite corner. You will have a strip with a wide point at both ends.

2. Use scissors to round the end points.

3. Color and decorate the shrink plastic with permanent markers, ink, and rubber stamps.

4. Place the colored shrink plastic in the box and heat it slowly with the heat gun.

5. When the plastic lays flat again, it is fully shrunk.

6. To shape the bracelet, press it completely flat with a flat object, such as the back of a rubber stamp.

7. Reheat the bracelet fully, until the plastic is limp. Working quickly, gently pick up the bracelet with the tweezers or hot pad, lay it over the round bottle, and wrap it around. You will probably need to reheat different sections to get the bracelet to fully wrap around the bottle. The plastic will be hot, so use caution, tweezers, and the hot pad while wrapping the bracelet.

8. To ruffle the cuff, you essentially stretch the plastic repeatedly along the edge. Heat a 1" to 2" (2.5 to 5 cm) section at a time and, using the tweezers or hot pad, ruffle the section. Repeat along the entire cuff edge.

9. To add the glitter effect, brush a thin layer of the pearl mica flakes over different areas of the bracelet.

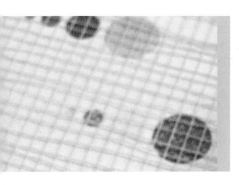

# *Rolled and Pressed:*

## Paper Clay Necklace

## Materials

**Basic Paper Tool Kit**

**Basic Jewelry Tool Kit**

**fluid acrylic paints**

**paper clay**

**paper towels**

**rubber stamps**

**acrylic gel (gloss)**

**three bead holder pendants**

**three jump rings**

**ready-to-finish necklace base**

IF YOU'VE NEVER WORKED WITH PAPER CLAY, I ENCOURAGE YOU TO give it a try. It's tintable, moldable, forgiving, and, well, it will make you feel like a kid again. Did I mention how easy it is to work with? For this project, we're going back to basics and rolling beads—long one, short ones, and even little bitty ones. And, because this is a book on altered paper, we're even going to alter our paper beads. By mixing small amounts of fluid acrylics into the clay, we can change the color of the beads. Then we can press them into rubber stamps and let them dry overnight before altering them again with fluid acrylics and acrylic gel. The bead holders for this necklace allow you to change your beads over and over again, making it customizable on a daily basis.

1. Knead one or two drops of paint into small pieces of paper clay to change the color. This is a messy undertaking, so keep your work space covered and paper towels handy.

2. Roll beads into different shapes, then press them against detailed rubber stamps to transfer the texture to the beads.

3. To create the bead holes, push an awl halfway through each paper bead, then turn the bead over and push the awl through from the opposite end. This keeps the beads from becoming misshapen.

4. Let the beads dry overnight.

5. Mix a little fluid acrylic paint with the acrylic gel and rub into and around the crevices of the beads. The color will sit in the crevices, and the rest of the piece will remain shiny. Let the beads dry.

6. Attach the dried beads to the bead holder pendants.

7. Use **jump rings** (page 16) to attach the bead holder pendants to the necklace base.

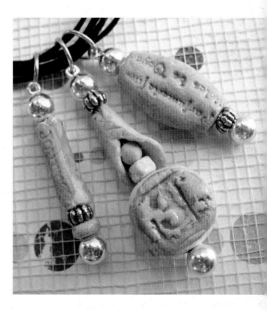

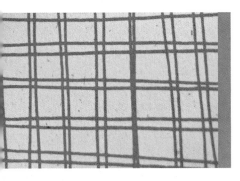

# Wistful Thinking:
## Paper Clay Variation

## Materials

**Basic Paper Tool Kit**

**Basic Jewelry Tool Kit**

**fluid acrylic paints**

**paper clay**

**paper towels**

**detailed rubber stamps**

**acrylic gel (gloss)**

**¾" (3 cm) and ½" (1.6 cm) ribbons**

**watch kit**

**two jump rings**

**lobster clasp**

PLAYING WITH PAPER CLAY HELPS YOU GET A FEEL FOR IT, WHICH will aid you in making the beads and watch parts for this watch. Creating the shank part of the bead is tricky, but don't give up. Remember that you can always ball the clay back up and start again. You could also string a series of these beads together to create a bracelet, sans watch, or make just one to hang as a lovely pendant. With a little patience, you may just find that paper clay is your new favorite studio supply.

1. Knead one or two drops of paint into a 1" (2.5 cm) ball of paper clay to change the color. This is a messy undertaking, so keep your work space covered and paper towels handy.

2. Divide the ball in half and press one of the halves onto a flat surface, so that you have a flat bead with a slightly rounded back.

3. Use a bone folder to gently press down most of the back and create a central arch along the back of the bead. With a bone folder or awl, pierce through this arch to create a bead-wide shank for the ribbon to go through.

4. Carefully press the smooth side of the bead against the detailed rubber stamps to transfer the texture. Repeat with the second half of the clay.

5. Let the beads dry overnight.

6. Mix a little fluid acrylic paint with the acrylic gel and rub it into and around the crevices of the bead. The color will sit in the crevices, and the rest of the piece will remain shiny. Let the beads dry.

7. String a double layer of ribbon through one bead, the watch face shanks, and then the second bead.

8. Tie an **overhand knot** (page 16) on the outside of the two beads, to hold them in place against the watch face.

9. Trim the ends of the ribbon to fit your wrist and **crimp** (page 17) the watch kit end findings onto the ends.

10. Add a **jump ring** (page 16) to both ends and a lobster clasp to one of the jump rings.

# Rebel with a Cuff:
## Fabric Paper Cuff-let

## Materials

**Basic Paper Tool Kit**

**Basic Jewelry Tool Kit**

**fabric scraps**

**sewing machine and/or needle and thread**

**computer and inkjet printer**

**inkjet-printable fabric paper**

**decorative-edge sewing scissors**

**felt**

**rubber stamps**

**permanent ink**

**pins**

**two blank bracelet bands**

ALTHOUGH THIS PROJECT USES TWO BIG MACHINES—A COMPUTER AND a sewing machine—it can easily be adapted for the sewing machine–phobic and noncomputer–savvy crafter. By simply using a needle and thread and alphabet or other stamps to print the message, you can make one of these indie artist–inspired cuff-lets without plugging in a thing. By adjusting the buckles on the bracelet bands, the cuff can easily be made bigger or smaller, which makes this project a great gift. The bracelet bands are also easy to remove, making it possible to interchange them with any number of fabric cuff-lets. And, because the fabric swatches needed for this project are so small, you can even substitute a wide ribbon, instead. Any way you stitch it, this is a cuff-let that you'll love on your wrist.

1. Cut two fabric scraps to 2¾" × 6" (7 cm × 15 cm).

2. Place the fabric scraps right sides together and sew around the perimeter (¼" [6 mm] from the edge), leaving a gap to turn the fabric right-side out. Use a needle and thread to sew up the gap after turning.

3. Print your message or photo onto the fabric paper and cut out the message. (The final size should be 2" × 5¼" [5 cm × 13 cm].)

4. Use the decorative-edge sewing scissors to cut the felt into a rectangle slightly larger than the fabric paper piece.

5. Use the rubber stamps and permanent ink to embellish the fabric paper, then remove the paper backing.

6. Layer the sewn fabric scraps with the felt piece, place the embellished fabric paper on top, and pin to hold the layers together.

7. Sew along the outside edge of the long side of the layers. Lift the sewing foot, turn the fabric around, and sew back in the direction you just sewed, over the previous stitching. Don't worry about lining up the stitches.

8. Stitch along the other long edge, repeating the instructions for step 7.

9. Sew a long rectangle shape down the middle of the layers, leaving enough room for the two bracelet bands. Stitch over the rectangle a second time.

10. Remove the pins and insert the bracelet bands.

11. Fray the edge of the fabric paper and trim any loose threads.

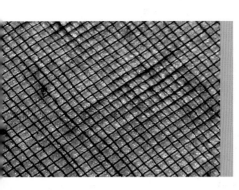

# London Neckline:
## Fabric Paper Variation

## Materials

**Basic Paper Tool Kit**

**Basic Jewelry Tool Kit**

**computer and inkjet printer**

**inkjet-printable fabric paper**

**permanent markers**

**alphabet stamps**

**rubber stamps**

**permanent ink**

**fluid acrylic paints**

**paintbrush**

**sewing machine and/or needle and thread**

**Golden GAC 400 (stiffens textiles)**

**acrylic gel (gloss)**

**book text**

**Crop-a-Dile or other eyelet-setting tool**

**two copper eyelets**

**20-gauge copper wire**

**necklace wire**

THE ABILITY TO PRINT ONTO FABRIC IMMEDIATELY LED ME TO THE idea of using photos in a piece of jewelry. This pendant is the outcome. By mixing my paper-altering supplies with photographs printed on fabric paper, I was able to make a quilted, painted, stamped, and gelled piece of jewelry that serves as a miniature journal keepsake of a European vacation—and a really cool conversation piece! A simple hoop necklace makes this pendant interchangeable on the days I feel like "remembering" a little closer to home. Use photographs of a favorite pet, vacation spot, loved one, flower, or even a drawing for other necklace variations.

1. Print a black and white photograph onto the fabric paper.

2. Color sections of the photo with permanent markers.

3. Stamp and paint the image as desired.

4. Cut out the image, leaving room at the top for eyelets, then cut two more pieces of fabric paper the same size. (To make the necklace reversible, repeat the same printing and decorating procedure with a second piece.)

5. With the decorated piece on top, stack the three pieces of fabric. (Place the second decorated piece, right-side out, on the bottom, if you're making a reversible necklace.) With a sewing machine, loosely sew around the perimeter of the stack (alternatively, you can hand stitch around the edges).

6. Paint two thin layers of the GAC 400 over the fabric within the sewing perimeter and let dry.

7. Use the acrylic gel to adhere and seal the book text to the front of the piece.

8. Punch two holes and add two eyelets for hanging the pendent.

9. Cut two 3" (7.5 cm) pieces of copper. Fold them in half and make a **double loop** on each end (page 14). Push the ends together, then string the pendant onto a necklace wire.

CHAPTER

6

# *Anthology of Adornment*

THIS IS THE CHAPTER YOUR MUSE HAS BEEN WAITING FOR—THE DESSERT COURSE in a glorious banquet of personal ornamentation. Whether you bought this book to inspire your own creations or to help you understand the mechanics of new projects, this chapter is the gravy. How do I know this? I, too, was touched and changed by each piece when it arrived at my studio. From the simplicity of Jennifer Francis Bitto's pendant (page 103) to the meticulous creation from Francesca Vitali of Frucci Design (page 92), each piece has something to offer.

Enjoy this chapter as you would a conversation with a good friend. Savor it and be challenged by it. If you are a jeweler, take in the different mixed-media techniques that these artists bring to the table: Kelli Perkins' recycled compact disk and paper bead pins (page 110), for example, or the whimsical fine art embodied in the collage pins of fred free (page 104). If your background is mixed media, be influenced by the construction of Catherine Moore's ethereal earrings (page 94) and the beautiful simplicity of Betsy Siber's work (page 93).

Enjoy!

# Perle e nodi [necklace] and Coupy cubetto [earrings]

**by Francesca Vitali of Frucci Design**

Recycled paper, pearls, nylon thread, handmade sterling silver clasp.

*Francesca says her design aims at valorizing common materials and transforming them into precious objects. In the necklace specifically, she wanted to emphasize and, at the same time, blend the opposite characteristics of the recycled paper and the noble pearls.*

# Vintage Postal Stamp Ensemble

**by Betsy Siber**

Vintage postage stamps, card stock, laminate, sterling silver jewelry findings, seed beads (earrings).

*Made from postmarked stamps from around the world, Betsy's pieces are small samples of history, design, and culture.*

## Robin Earrings [earrings]
## C-a-t-h-e-r-i-n-e Name Bracelet [bracelet]

**by Catherine Moore**

Acrylic decoupage, jewelry findings, letter tiles, wood disks, beads, charms, stamps.

*Inspired by natural elements, Catherine finds unique and beautiful ways to incorporate her passion into her jewelry pieces.*

# Parlez-Vous Oiseau Brooch [bird]
# Keep a Tree in Your Heart Brooch [tree]

**by Catherine Moore**

Jewelry findings, paper, charms.

*A clever choice of images and embellishments makes this a pair of enticing brooches.*

# Orbit Necklace
## by Tracy Belair Gaito

Paper beads, sterling silver jewelry findings, blue topaz bead, silver bead chain.

*This necklace took shape as Tracy experimented with a collection of paper beads created from long, tightly rolled and sculpted strips of paper. Each paper bead is approximately ½˝ (1 cm) in diameter.*

## Pink Caddilackadaisical Necklace

**by Joanna Taylor**

Hand-dyed paper, glue, varnish, beading wire, beads, lime chalk, crimp beads, sterling silver wire.

*A Florida prom queen, hopped up on caffeine and headed for the beach—partially controlled mayhem.
Joanna loves making bold jewelry that is elegant yet displays a sense of humor.*

# Winter Garden Art Deco Necklace and Earrings
**by Anita Byers**

Paper, adhesive, jump rings, ear wires, punches, rhinestones, ribbon, foam dots.

*Influenced by her love of paper and collage, Anita fashioned this necklace and earring ensemble with Art Deco flair.*

# Butterfly Magic Pin and Earrings
**by Anita Byers**

Paper, adhesive, rhinestones, ink, pin back, earring wires.

*Glitter, rhinestones, and a butterfly swirl around these "magical" jewelry pieces.*

# Birds of a Feather Earrings

**by Rochelle Bourgault**

Paper, jewelry findings, beads.

*If folding the proverbial 1,000 cranes is beyond the scope of your ambition (and fine-motor skills), creating this pair of earrings will usher in enough luck, for as long as you're wearing them. These earrings are assembled from tiny origami cranes, whose wings flap with a gentle tug of the tail, and a few cleverly placed findings. Substitute any number of folded figures for endless wardrobe options … and conversation pieces.*

# Orchid Headband

## by Linda Blinn

Headband, paper, florist tape and wire, beads, adhesive, trim, ink.

*This versatile headband could comfortably show up at events from luaus to weddings. Making their own versions would keep the girlie girls (of any age) busy at a party. Add ribbons and "jewels" to glam it up for Halloween, costume parties, or flower fairy fantasies.*

## Paper Doll Necklace

**by Lisa Guerin**

Card stock, cardboard, stamp, ink, colored pencils, crepe paper, string, eyelets, adhesive.

*Designing and creating paper dolls has become Lisa's most cherished obsession. Always looking for fun new ways to enjoy her little paper doll, Lisa was encouraged to put her on a necklace. Now she can travel everywhere!*

# Collage and Silver Necklace
## by Jennifer Francis Bitto

Ribbon, metal frame, paper, stamp, ink, die cuts.

*Jennifer's combination of beautiful ribbon, distressed silver frame, and collage art forms a lovely locket-like jewel for a neckline embellishment.*

## was before [hands and clock], radiating signals [girl and boy], fred found [man with glasses]

**by fred free**

Found text and images, colored pencil, adhesive, slide glass, bar pin, ball chain.

*Images and text were glued to all but the top layer of slide glass to create a sense of three-dimensionality within an otherwise two-dimensional collage. Inspiration for Fred's work comes from a love of small, random, and seemingly meaningless moments in life.*

# Her Creative Slip Is Showing Pendant

**by Allison Strine Designs**

Collage, glass, soldering supplies.

*Allison combines her contemplative side with her not-so-serious side when creating Lady Bird pendants such as this one.*

## Cameo Necklace

**by Barbara Smith**

Paper, rubber stamps, colored pencils, Diamond Glaze, metal frame, photo hooks, vintage necklace, small rhinestone, glue.

*For this lovely necklace, Barbara used paper to create a cameo-type piece with a vintage feel.*

## If Flowers Could Talk Pins

**by Paula Guerin**

Cardboard flower form, bubble wrap, paper, matte medium, clip art or stamped faces, embellishments, lace, sequins, copper tape, mesh fabric, rickrack, shelf paper transfers.

*Paula loves wearing vintage pins and finds many of them at garage sales. She especially enjoys flower pins from the '60s and '70s. Paula also loves working with women's faces in many of her collages, because she feels that they create instant mood, almost as if they could communicate emotions.*

## "?!&" Collection

**by Kristen Poissant**

Paper, coloring agent, adhesive, jewelry base.

*The "?!&" Collection is a study of the many unique forms created from a number of recognizable novelty typefaces. Each piece of type creates a form that is its own piece of art.*

## Chain Link Bracelet

**by Yetunde Rodriguez**

Magazine images, resin, embellishments, Mod Podge, jump rings, toggle clasp.

*Yetunde loves using objects for non-intended purposes, and when she saw these paper crafting embellishments in the store, they just begged her to be repurposed.*

# Recycled Junk Mail Pins

**by Kelli Perkins**

Recycled compact disk, acrylic paint, black poster board, papers, embossing ink, clear ultra-thick embossing enamel, embossing powder, gold leaf, plastic straw, small dowel rod, copper wire, pin finding.

*Making junk mail into art is a great way to recycle those bothersome fliers and compact disks. Hold the CDs under hot water to soften them for cutting, then layer on paper mosaic pieces, gold leaf, wire, and paper beads made from unwanted advertisements. You'll never look at junk mail the same way again!*

## Art Deco Joy Pin
**by Anita Byers**

Paper, adhesive rhinestones, pin back, punches, cardboard.

*A little glitz, a little rhinestone, and a little dimension were all it took for Anita to make this eye-catching brooch.*

## Cell Phone Bling
**by Jami Petersen**

Laser-cut paper shapes, paper hardener, adhesive-backed rhinestones, jewelry wire.

*Jewelry isn't just for your body—why not bling up your cell phone with these paper shapes? In fact, most phones come equipped for these cute little accessories; just slip the wire through the opening and you're ready to show off.*

# Tea Time Brooch [teapot girl]
# Petite Marie Paper Brooch [woman with birds]
## by Catherine Moore

Ribbon, lace, buttons, stamps, vintage millinery.

*Catherine likes to refer to her paper doll pieces, such as these two brooches, as her "paper confections."*

## Bird & Bead Pendant

**by Deborah Costolloe**

Bamboo bead, photograph printed on matte paper, photo-editing software, beads, adhesive, necklace base.

*This pendant combines two of my favorite mediums: photos and beads. The original photograph of a bird figurine on a branch was transformed into a pen and ink drawing with photo-editing software.*

## Meadowlark Pendant [bird], Home Sweet Nest Pendant [bird house]

**by Catherine Moore**

Tag, paint, stamp, brass charm, ribbon.

*Catherine's quick and delightful tag pendants can not only hang around your neck but can also be used as a beautiful package, vase, or memo board embellishment.*

# Contributing Artists

## Jennifer Francis Bitto

has worked in the paper crafting industry for the past fourteen years as a magazine editor, an artist, an author, and a teacher. She loves to share her paper passion with anyone willing to pick up a rubber stamp or pair of scissors. Her books with coauthors Jenn Mason and Linda Blinn are *Celebrating Baby* and *Handmade Gifts* (both from Rockport). She can be reached at Franciepantz@yahoo.com.

## Linda Blinn

is a former magazine editor and the author of *Making Family Journals*. She also coauthored *Celebrating Baby* and *Handmade Gifts*. Linda is currently designing products for the craft industry and teaching classes on art journaling and mixed-media surface design for home decor. She lives in San Clemente, California.

## Rochelle Bourgault

aspires to pithiness but errs toward the verbose. She is an all-around crafty freelance writer, who is inspired by vintage photographs, winter sunrises, and opportune puns, depending on the time of day. She lives in Salem, Massachusetts, and is the author of *Hip Graphic Knits* (Quarry 2006). See her work at www.onepartmoxie.com or send her a note at rochelle.bourgault@gmail.com.

## Anita Byers

has been playing with paper since her childhood paper doll days. She truly believes that paper dolls are her art of choice. After starting a job at the Artbar in Santa Ana, California, her world expanded artistically, and she has been experimenting more in her collage work. Anita has been married for thirty-three years and has enthusiastically reached sixty years of age. "Pass me the glue and paper—I've got work to do!"

## Deborah Costolloe

enjoys a life-long love of beads, photography, and craft. She can be reached at Deborah.Costolloe@comcast.net.

## fred free

cuts and pastes and wonders why in Brookline, Massachusetts, with his wife and son and rather large plastic deer. His work can be found at www.fredfree.com.

## Tracy Belair Gaito

lives in the wooded hills of Huntington, Vermont. She has been interested in art and crafts since she was little, drawing horses before Saturday morning cartoons, crafting tiny books about Quacky, her pet duck, and weaving baskets of rope and yarn. As a grown-up, Tracy likes her work to lean toward the stylistic and abstract, her love of punchy color schemes figuring heavily in her designs. When not rolling paper and covered in glue, Tracy is a graphic designer with her own business. She loves the creative life she shares with her musician husband and their two cats (who are not very creative but provide endless hours of entertainment and sometimes eat her paper art). See Tracy's work online at www.runnerbeanarts.com and runnerbean.etsy.com, or send her a note at runnerbeanarts@gmail.com.

## Lisa Guerin

is a self-taught mixed-media scrap artist living in Southern California. Lisa enjoys life with husband Rick, son Brandon, and kitty Sophie. You can check out her art and follow her art adventures by reading her blog at http://lisaguerin-artblog.blogspot.com.

## Paula Guerin

has always been driven by the creative spirit. She loves the creative process and enjoys immersing herself in almost any design project. For her, a collage is a sort of puzzle of emotions, putting together parts to create a mood. You can e-mail Paula at aqua-marine@earthlink.net or visit her at www.paulatguerin.com to learn more.

## Catherine Moore

is a conceptual artist, product designer, wife, mother to two sons and three cats, big sister, and daughter. She strives for balance between nurturing her family and expressing herself as an individual. She is drawn to old-fashioned archetypal imagery, such as the objects that are part of our daily lives at home: laundry pins, hangers, spoons, cups, and saucers. Because of her connection to the natural world, over time, her metaphors evolved, with birds, nests, eggs, and feathers forming the foundation of her visual language. Catherine might be best known for her whimsical line of rubber stamps, Character Constructions, in which women can be teapots and men have been known to employ unorthodox modes of travel, including in teacups and on the backs of birds. Catherine works from her home-based studio in Peachtree City, Georgia. Visit her at PostoDel-Sol@aol.com and www.CharacterConstructions.com.

## Kelli Perkins

is a mixed-media artist who turns common life into art as Ephemeral Alchemy. She's a frequent contributor to *Cloth Paper Scissors* magazine, and when she's not creating, she's peddling information as the head reference librarian of her local public library. Most of her work incorporates book text, a fitting symbol of her passion for language and literature. Contact her at kelliperkins@charter.net or visit her gallery at kelliperkins.blogspot.com.

## Jami Petersen

is the editor for *Scrapbooking.com Magazine*. She contributes many articles and is also responsible for the weekly newsletter, which brims with tips and ideas for every paper crafter. Sign up to receive them in your e-mail at www.scrapbooking.com. Jami also designs for the online program Scrapbook Lounge. Her webisodes are accessible twenty-four hours a day, seven days a week. You can see her in action at www.tvweekly.com. Jami lives in San Diego, California, and can be reached at jamipeaches@yahoo.com.

## Kristen Poissant

is a full-time graphic designer and typographer who daydreams of creating cheeky and fun designs that inspire and delight. She creates all of her designs out of her little New York City apartment, which has a fabulous view. In early 2007, she opened her very first design shop, kapcity, through the wonderful online marketplace of handmade items, Etsy. In the future, kapcity will expand its line of products and artwork. Many surprises are still to come. Visit her at www.kapcity.etsy.com and www.kapcity.blogspot.com.

## Yetunde Rodriguez

was born and partly raised in Nigeria, West Africa. She has always loved making things, ever since her mom gave her a book titled *How to Make Things for Fun*. Arriving in the United States in 1985, she remembers being awed by the abundance of craft materials available. It would be many more years before she surrendered to her crafting passion, in lieu of a "real" career. After coming to the realization that she wouldn't be a doctor as her family had hoped, Yetunde majored in graphic design at Hampton University. She loves most crafts but prefers to make something utilitarian, rather than something just to look at. She also loves sewing, baking, soap making, knitting, and crocheting. Yetunde is currently a stay-at-home mom of three and a freelance graphic designer. She also sells her wares at craft shows and on Etsy. Visit her at http://jesplayin.etsy.com, http://thraftychic.wordpress.com and www.myspace.com/taiwosoaps.

## Betsy Siber

was born in 1983 and grew up in South Bend, Indiana. After graduating from Columbia College, Chicago, with a bachelor of arts in photography in 2005, she started creating jewelry under the name Foxglove Accessories. With a background in photography, bookbinding, printmaking, graphic design, and paper arts, she creates pieces made from found and recycled objects in Chicago, Illinois. Her work can be found online at Etsy and in boutiques across the country. Visit FoxgloveAccessories.com for more information, including stores, upcoming shows, and new designs, or e-mail her at Foxgloveaccessories@gmail.com

## Barbara Smith

has enjoyed art for as long as she can remember.
She still has fond memories of attending art classes
as a young girl and trying many different arts and
crafts as a young adult. During a visit to Texas a
few years back, Barbara's sister-in-law introduced
her to the art of creating scrapbooks. This was the
springboard for her exploration of paper arts and the
perfect way to incorporate her love of photos, new
and old, into her art. Barbara loves making cards,
creating scrapbook pages, and altering books and
various other objects. She especially loves collage.
In addition to creating art, she is employed full
time in the computer industry. Barbara resides with
her husband and daughter in South Florida. Visit
her at http://smith411.typepad.com or contact her
at smith2236@bellsouth.net.

## Allison Strine

by day, is a happy mixed-media collage artist
whose exuberant creations have won awards and
appeared in national arts magazines. By night, she
is a not-very-good cook, a wife to a right-brained
husband (or is it the left—the one that's all about
math and none about art), and a tucker-inner of two
glorious children. See her work at allisonstrine.etsy.
com or write her at allisonstrine@mac.com.

## Joanna Taylor

is a trained linguist with a deep love for making
objects that celebrate self-expression and language.
Influenced by calligraphic traditions, mosaics, and
whimsical modern design, she combines her long-
standing passions for the written word, paper arts,
and jewelry making to create vibrant wearable art.
My Word! Jewelry was born out of a desire to play
with all the things she likes to play with, all at the
same time, and a desire to make something with
her hands that everyone can take pleasure in. Raised
on a sailboat in coastal Florida, Joanna currently
lives in Indiana with two cats, two turtles, and a
philosopher. Visit her at www.mywordjewelry.com
or contact her at mywordjewelry@gmail.com.

## Francesca Vitali

was born in Italy, where she studied chemistry at
the University "LaSapienza" in Rome. She moved
to Switzerland for her PhD in organic chemistry and
now works at the University of California, Irvine.
Parallel to running her scientific experiments,
Francesca developed her artistic path. Eventually
she found herself transforming paper into precious
objects, realizing that she'd become an alchemist.
See her work at www.fruccidesign.com or contact her
at fruccidesign@gmail.com.

# *Templates*

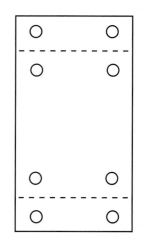

WRIST RINGLET: LAMINATED PAPER
VARIATION TEMPLATE

MOOD SWINGS: LAMINATED PAPER
PENDANT TEMPLATE

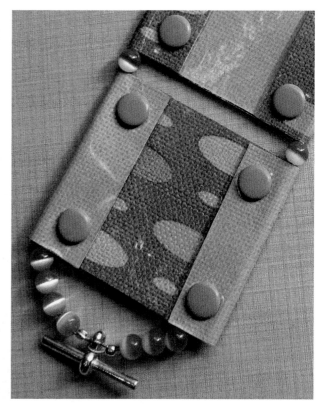

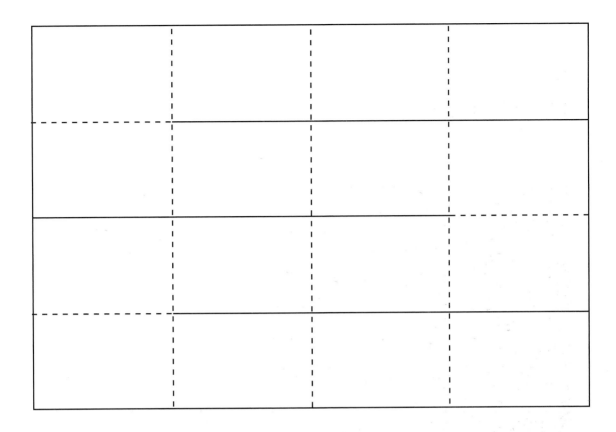

A TRIP REMEMBERED: MINI JOURNAL
NECKLACE TEMPLATE

FINGER RAPT: SHRINK PLASTIC
RING TEMPLATE

IT'S EASY BEING GREEN: MINI JOURNAL
VARIATION TEMPLATE

*Appendix*

## Origami Lilies

1. With main color facing down, mountain fold and unfold the paper square diagonally in both directions.

2. With the main color facing down, valley fold and unfold the paper in half vertically and horizontally.

3. Refold the paper in half horizontally and push the two outside bottom corners in toward the center.

4. Keep pushing until all four corners meet in the middle.

5. Flatten the model by moving two flaps to the right and two flaps to the left.

6. Turn the model, so that the raw edges point toward you.

*Continued on next page*

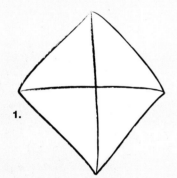

1.

2.

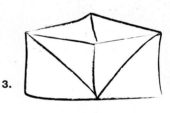

3.

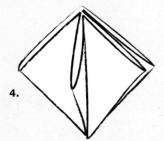

4.

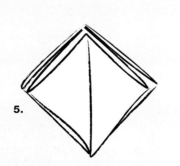

5.

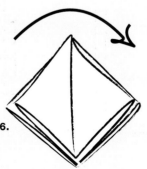

6.

## Origami Lilies (cont.)

7. Lift one flap up so that it is perpendicular to the work surface.

8. Insert your finger into the flap.

9. Slowly press the flap flat.

10. Fold the flap to the side and repeat steps 8 and 9 with the other three flaps, to form a kite shape.

11. With the flattened fold facing you, fold the bottom raw edges in to the center crease and unfold.

12. Carefully lift the raw edge on the top center of the model away from you.

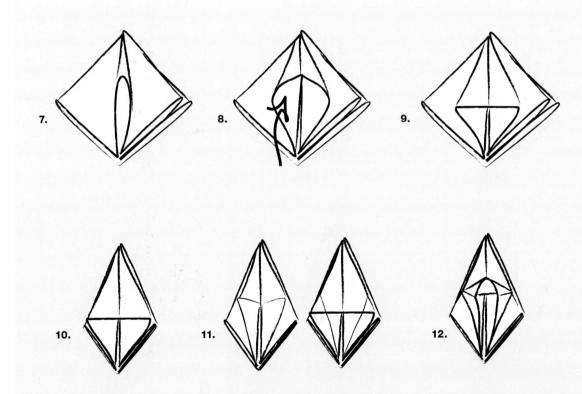

7.    8.    9.

10.    11.    12.

# Origami Lilies (cont.)

13. Repeat steps 11 and 12 for all four sides.

14. Turn the shape 180°, so that the open points face away from you.

15. Fold all four of the triangular flaps away from you.

16. Flip the layers around, so that a plain diamond shape is facing up.

17. Fold the bottom edge of the smooth diamond up to the center crease. Repeat with all four sides.

18. Pull the opposite points apart to open the model and create the petals. Repeat with the other two petals. Round the petals over a pencil or a brush handle to shape.

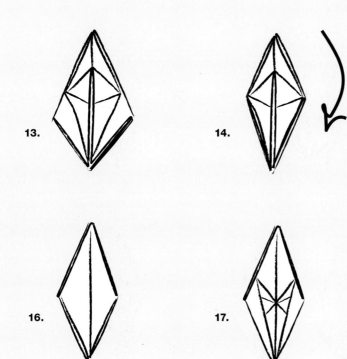

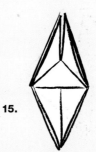

13.

14.

15.

16.

17.

18.

# Resources

**A.C. Moore**
www.acmoore.com

**A Country Welcome**
www.acountrywelcome.com
*The place to find cool products such as the drilled dominoes used in the Domino Effect and Mini Mélange.*

**A Guide to Bead Work**
www.guidetobeadwork.com
*Looking for a bead store near you? This is the site to visit. A fairly extensive compilation of bead stores around the world.*

**Archiver's**
www.archiversonline.com

**Blue Moon Beads**
www.creativityinc.com
*Beads and jewelry-making supplies (available at Michaels Stores).*

**Character Constructions**
www.characterconstructions.com
*A great place to look for unique papers, stamps, images d'art, and decoration.*

**Cousin Corporation of America**
A Touch of Glass
www.cousin.com
*A great source for fabulous beads available at retailers in all fifty states and several countries outside of the United States.*

**Crafts Etc!**
www.craftsetc.com
*Jewelry-making basics. Order online.*

**Creativity Inc.**
DMD/Autumn Leaves
www.creativityinc.com
*Great source for beautiful papers and embellishments.*

**Crystal Innovations™**
www.pureallure.com
*Crystals and classy jewelry-making supplies, such as the watch face kit used in Wristful Thinking.*

**Darice**
www.darice.com
*Jewelry-making staples. Check the website for online ordering information.*

**Halcraft USA, Inc.**
Bead Heaven
www.halcraft.com
*Great jewelry-making findings, such as eyeglass cord kits (available at major craft store chains).*

**Hancock Fabrics Online Fabric Store**
www.hancockfabrics.com

## Hirschberg Schutz and Co.

Hirschberg Decorative Details
Jewelry & Craft Essentials
650 Liberty Avenue, Union, NJ 07083
ph: (908) 810-1111
fax: (908) 810-7218
*Lots and lots of jewelry-making supplies (available at Michaels Stores).*

## JoAnn Fabric and Craft Stores

www.joann.com

## Lightning Colors

www.lightningcolors.com
*Chandelier crystals that will make you drool. Great colors, too!*

## Making Memories

www.makingmemories.com
*Hip, happening paper art and scrapbook supplies. Order online or check the site to find a supplier near you.*

## Michaels

www.michaels.com

## Museum of Useful Things

www.themut.com
*Fun store to shop at in person (Cambridge, MA) or online. Find the display clips for the mood swing necklace—among other cool things—here.*

## Off the Beaded Path

www.beyondthebeadedpath.com/index3.html
*Because I had to put at least one awesome "destination" bead store on the resource list. Beautiful beads and jewelry supplies and a great staff. Located in Great Barrington, MA.*

## One Heart One Mind

www.oneheart-onemind.com
*The perfect online store for buckles and other acrylic shapes.*

## Paper Source

www.papersource.com
*One of my favorite stores to browse, but you can order online, too. Several U.S. locations.*

## The Pear Tree

www.thepeartreeofbrookline.com
*As a dedicated patron of small, independently-owned stores, I had to also mention my new haunt, The Pear Tree, a full-service bead store located in the heart of Coolidge Corner in Brookline, Massachusetts.*

## Prym Consumer USA

Dritz
www.dritz.com
*Reliable provider of sewing goodies, such as buckles and printable fabric paper (available at Jo-Ann Stores).*

## Tandy Leather Factory

www.tandyleatherfactory.com
*Order everything from buckle blanks to belt kits here (also available at Michaels Stores).*

# About the Author

*J*ENN MASON IS A WHIMSICAL DO-ER AND OUTSIDE-THE-BOX THINKER who is especially fond of sharing her love of living creatively. She has coauthored two books and authored another four in the midst of developing new products, writing a column for *Cloth Paper Scissors* magazine, and carrying out a fine art career.

When she's not out beautifying the craft world with inventive new product design (or playing games with her daughters, or driving to Irish dancing class, or....), you can probably find her in the studio of her newly renovated 150-year-old carriage house—which still had horse stalls in it when she started this book. Jenn's home and studio, sans stalls, is in Brookline, Massachusetts. Catch her regularly on her website: www.JennMason.com.

Other books by Jenn Mason:

- Pockets, Pull-outs, and Hiding Places
- Paper Art Workshop: Handmade Gifts
- Paper Art Workshop: Celebrating Baby
- Art of the Family Tree
- The Cardmaker's Workbook

# Acknowledgments

THERE IS NEVER ENOUGH TIME OR SPACE TO THANK EVERYONE WHO helped me with writing my books, but I'd be remiss not to thank my most stupendous, understanding, helpful, honest, and generous editor, Mary Ann Hall. Thanks also to Pat Price and the many other hands at Quayside who helped make this light work—and for inviting me to the crafting soirees.

Thanks to the amazingly talented artists who created the marvelous pieces for the gallery section under abbreviated time constraints and with such a positive attitude toward the challenge.

Thanks must also go out to Martha, Eileen, Karin, Deborah, Jen, John, the So. Cal. Crew, and all my other friends both near and far for watching my kids, providing me with stimulating conversation, challenging my status quo, going on research (a.k.a. shopping) expeditions with me, putting up with me, and being the kind of people who make this (and my) world a better place.

Thanks to Rob and the Stealth Construction crew for building my most amazing new home and studio in the midst of writing this book. Having the right place to work is just as important as having the right tools.

And finally, thanks to the Love-o-My-Life trio, Matt, Becky, and Abby. Thanks for making this life of mine so complete. I endeavor to make you proud—always.